"Speckhardt boldly warns of the insi[...] theocrats. Drawing from science, hist[...] convincingly makes case that humanity[...] it embraces the humanist creed of emp[...] thinking. It is an essential book of our ti[...] [...]ogressive message at our peril."

—**Robyn Blumner**, executive director of the Richard Dawkins Foundation for Reason and Science and CEO of the Center for Inquiry

"This book is a superb introduction to humanism for the 21st century reader. Clearly presented and unusually concise, it's packed with compelling examples of humanism's historical and contemporary accomplishments—social, cultural, and political. In addition, it answers virtually any question a humanist, or potential humanist, might have in order to be better informed about this dynamic progressive movement."

—**Dr. Leon Seltzer, PhD**, psychologist, author, and blogger for *Psychology Today*

"Many people believe that if we could 'imagine no religion' we would have no foundation for the decisions we need to make about how to treat one another, the Earth, and the non-human beings we share it with. Many people don't know there is a God-free—if not values free—worldview. Humanism provides that guiding philosophy, and I can think of no better guide to modern humanism than this book. I learned a lot, and so will you."

—**Eugenie C. Scott, PhD**, physical anthropologist and founding executive director of the National Center for Science Education

"A thoughtful, thorough, and engaging invitation to humanism. Those of us who reject religion need to simultaneously affirm and advance the humanist values that we do believe in. Speckhardt's book offers an admirably clear and passionate articulation of those values, and how those values can work towards progressive change."

—**Phil Zuckerman, PhD**, author of *Faith No More: Why People Reject Religion* and professor of sociology at Pitzer College

"This little book is a rich compendium of philosophical arguments, vignettes, and FAQ's. Speckhardt not only makes a convincing case for a life guided by reason in the service of compassion, he also gives you practical tips about spreading the message. It will particularly appeal to those who feel attracted by humanism but are not quite there as yet."

—**Pervez Hoodbhoy, PhD**, nuclear physicist and writer

"The erudite history of a movement, a reasoned case for the propositions of modern Humanism, an urgent call to action, an engaging personal story - Roy Speckhardt's compelling book is all of these and everyone will get a return from time spent in its pages."

—**Andrew Copson**, Chief Executive of the British Humanist Association and President of the International Humanist and Ethical Union

Creating Change
Through Humanism

CREATING
CHANGE
THROUGH
HUMANISM

ROY SPECKHARDT

If you can identify with any single label from both
categories (a) and (b) then you're a humanist.

ONE FROM A		ONE FROM B		
atheist • agnostic • bright • freethinker • godless • heathen • heretic • ignostic • infidel • naturalist • nonbeliever • none • nontheist • rationalist • secular • skeptic	+	▪ progressive activist ▪ liberal advocate ▪ loving libertarian ▪ conservative humanitarian ▪ empathetic reformer	=	**HUMANISM**

HUMANIST PRESS
WASHINGTON, DC

CONTENTS

For Maggie

Foreword

By Rebecca Newberger Goldstein

Until quite recently, I was unaware of the existence of the secular humanist community, organized around the values of rationality, free inquiry, and the right that each of us has to flourish in this life—which is the only life that any of us will ever get. Yes, I believed, with all my being, in these values. But, for me, the process of ratiocination that had brought me to my conclusions didn't connect me with any normative community, by which I mean a community grounded on shared values.

Instead I tended to think of normative communities as restricted to religious communities. I had been raised in one such community, and my journey out of it was private, solitary, and silent. In fact, for many decades after I'd internally severed all ties from the belief system into which I'd been born and indoctrinated, I dared not breathe a word of my internal dissent. I shied away from causing any discomfort to those closest to me, fearing that the rejection of their beliefs would be felt as a rejection of them, mutually painful and distancing. And my reluctance to cause such discomfort was surely compounded by the female "modesty" that had been pounded into my psyche, a modesty interpreted so broadly as to merge into self-effacement. Mine certainly is not the only religious tradition that asserts strict control over its women, the sartorial coverings heavy with the symbolism of disappearance. The sense that there is something shameful in the very state of being a female is quite effective in stifling demurral.

Nevertheless, demur I did, though ever so demurely. I found the books I needed to read, thought the thoughts I needed to think, and repeated the process. Read, reflect, repeat. I trained myself to go through the motions of observance as mindlessly as possible, even when they offended the conclusions at which I'd arrived. I sought my solace in the fact that, no matter how constrained my external behavior might be, nobody could assert his authority over the autonomy of an active mind. I reveled in that inviolable autonomy and told myself, for decades, that it was all that I required.

But of course it wasn't. Such bifurcation between one's inner and outer selves exacts its toll. The bloody inconvenience of the intrusive religious requirements, very onerous in the particular tradition in which I was raised, was the least of it. More serious was the profound loneliness of inhabiting a place of unvoiced convictions, forever foregoing the give-and-take promoted by mutual respect. For me, every proposition was first rigorously assessed before it was expressed, not only for its soundness but also for its possible potential to give offense. As time went on, and my thinking progressed, the proportion of propositions that failed to meet the second requirement began to preponderate. That's a lonely space in which to be confined.

But far more debilitating still was the damage rendered to my own sense of integrity. Yes, I could tell myself that I was behaving as I was out of compassion for others, and so the sacrifices I was making was eminently moral. And, too, I could be scrupulous, as I tried to be, in never professing beliefs I didn't possess, in keeping mum while I went through the motions. Still, my observance itself proclaimed assent to propositions I vehemently denied, and the clash between convictions and performative declarations gradually chipped away at my sense of personal integrity.

It's an interesting word, *integrity,* sharing its root with the words *integer,* meaning a whole number, and *integrate,* meaning to combine into a whole. In other words, this term that refers to a high level of moral achievement also speaks of wholeness. Is it possible to be a person of integrity while maintaining a radical bifurcation between one's outer and inner lives? And if that inner life should value, above all, rationality, free inquiry, and the right of us all to flourish to our fullest, then how can you keep silent as to the conclusions to which your rational free inquiry has brought you? How can you deny for yourself the right to flourish in the company of like-minded people who will not disapprove of you for subjecting your beliefs and actions to the standards of rational accountability? If you believe in the integrity of your conclusions then you must show them to the world, making the case for them not only by the arguments you hash out in the privacy of your own mind but by the life that you publicly lead.

In this book, one that wonderfully articulates the values around which the secular humanist community is organized, you will find Roy Speckhardt arguing similarly. My heart skipped a beat when I read the passage in which he addresses the person I used to be, the one who divorced herself from the rituals she kept, rationalizing her lack of integrity as a moral duty to others. Normative communities that demand such rationalization are not normative communities that we should honor, not with our words or actions or even our silence. Or as Roy writes:

> When you no longer need to feign an identity that isn't yours, you'll discover confidence and the ability to say, "This is who I am," and speak out on any issue that stirs your heart and mind. By announcing your presence, others will come out to you who you didn't previously know shared your nontheism. You'll finally be able to meet other nontheists and build relationships based on truth and honesty. You can love and be loved by people who know the real you. No matter what you've been told, that person deserves to see the light of day.

How I wish I might have read that passage decades ago, but how glad I am to read it today, for I know how needed it remains. I hope that this passage, together with all that Roy has written in these pages, reaches an audience that includes those still struggling with the contradictions and compromises that blighted my former life. I hope that his book will help them find their way to the sweet wholeness of integrity and will bring them into a normative community that has so much to give—to them, to me, and to the world at large.

Introduction

Do you think science matters more than dogma? Do you think this life is all we're going to get, so we need to make the most of it? Do you find that helping other humans in the here and now gives you well-being? Do you think common sense is more important than rules in ancient texts? Do you trust your experience and knowledge over those who claim a personal connection to their god?

Then, whether you recognized it before or not, you're probably a humanist!

Humanists and other freethinkers can unite to bring humanist ideas to the forefront, and that's true in the United States today as it hasn't been for decades, maybe ever. That's because today we're seeing a confluence in the streams of ideas that lead people to consider the merits of ethics derived from human need and interest rather than from archaic texts or divine revelation.

Some of the credit for this shift in thinking is due to those we're less inclined to thank. We've seen Religious Right leaders like Pat Robertson and Ralph Reed in the 1990s, followed by right-wing politicos like Tom DeLay, Rick Santorum, and the anti-intellectual George W. Bush, followed by new creationist/intelligent design advocates like Ken Ham and Sarah Palin, followed by tea partiers like Rand Paul and Michele Bachmann. Each of these people, by shoving their extreme beliefs in our faces at every turn, make a contribution to galvanizing us in our struggle for a more humanistic view. These agents of theocratism, who view secular humanists and atheists as in league with the devil, are spurs in the sides of those who would propel our ideas into the spotlight.

Another stream that raised consciousness found its source in the first outpouring of popular nontheist authors. Richard Dawkins, Sam Harris, Daniel Dennett, Ayaan Hirsi Ali, and Christopher Hitchens penned the first top-selling books challenging the taboos about criticizing traditional religious beliefs and questioning the existence of a god. This was a special breakthrough because in past decades, to publish a forthrightly nontheistic book, one needed to go through a freethought publisher. As recently as 2004, author Susan Jacoby noted that we've not seen broad popularity for nontheist authors since the late 1800s when a freethought orator like Robert G. Ingersoll could be widely appreciated. Later in 2004, the tide turned.

Popular humanist and atheist authors—who may have been writing all along—got a boost in interest as the rapidly growing number of nontheists looked for what was next. Perhaps they agreed with Dawkins that God was a delusion, but given that, what more could they learn about the world? That's when we saw Greg Epstein write about building humanist communities, Steven Pinker explain how we're progressing to a better world community, and the blogosphere light up with the modern ideas of Greta Christina, Seth Andrews, and Hemant Mehta.

Another stream was seen in the provocative humanist and atheist ad campaigns appearing on billboards and buses in big cities and major highways. The American Humanist Association (AHA) led the way in coordinated campaigns and was quickly joined by Freethought Action, Freedom From Religion Foundation, American Atheists, and the United Coalition of Reason. The campaigns typically cost just thousands of dollars, a fraction of the millions they earned in publicity through the overwhelmingly positive media coverage they received around the globe. And in cases where there was a legal fight about the right to post such ads, or the ads were vandalized, the publicity increased even more. Harder to quantify, however, was how these efforts were leading more to choose a this-worldly philosophy and be increasingly open about their choice.

The rise of social media and online information sources and the humanists' quick adoption of such outlets to gather likeminded people was also a significant stream. One study, using data from the General Social Survey and reported in 2014 through the Cornell

University Library, specifically found a significant direct correlation between Internet use and absence of religion. It appears that exposure to a broader base of ideas reveals the quaintness of holding to one faith as true while regarding all others are false. And it becomes apparent that the supernatural ideas varying from faith to faith are just human creations.

What's happening is telling. Camp Quest, a summer camp for freethinking kids, was for years a haven for just a couple dozen kids of humanist activist families. Suddenly, it now has over a thousand kids signed up and continues to rapidly add new camps. The idea for a National Day of Reason to counter the government-sponsored National Day of Prayer seemed modest in 2003, but today, with well over a hundred celebrations happening annually and cities and towns marking the day with official proclamations, momentum may be significant enough to turn the tide against government-sponsored prayer. Where once it was unthinkable for politicians and atheists to meet, now the Freethought Equality Fund PAC is funding campaigns at state and federal levels and getting regular audiences with dozens of members of Congress and other influential politicians. While we have two former US Representatives in Pete Stark and Barney Frank who came out as nontheists—Stark, while in office and Frank, after retirement—someday there will be many sitting members of Congress who are comfortable doing the same.

With all that changed in recent years and the influx of mainstream people into the humanist movement, it's past due time for a volume that is a plain-spoken modern introduction to humanism. That's the niche this effort aims to fill. It's only appropriate for such a book about contemporary humanism to not merely explain the ideas, but also call people to action. We have to create the humanistic change we'd like to see.

The first part of the book is foundational, beginning with Chapter One, which provides readers a basic overview of humanism and makes sure they have a chance to decide whether or not they are in fact humanists. Chapter Two further familiarizes readers with what is meant by humanism by describing the paths to humanism of three engaged humanists. Chapter Three provides an argument for humanism, not just for those who haven't adopted the humanist label, but as a tool for people to use as they see fit. It also seeks to encourage folks to be open about their identities. Chapter Four tells the story of humanism's beginnings and the rich history of the American Humanist Association. Chapter Five describes the challenges we face as humanists in a world resistant to nontheistic voices and reluctant to engage in progressive change. Chapter Six briefly outlines a vision of what we can achieve if we maintain our strength of conviction and apply it in effective action.

The second part of the book applies humanism to the modern world and recommends positions and courses of action.

The first chapter of Part Two looks at the political consequences of humanism, explaining how humanism isn't a knee-jerk liberal ideology but a considered worldview based on the best of what we've learned so far. Those political convictions are drawn from the application of the philosophy itself to modern issues and problems. After this is explained, there is a chapter on core humanist issues, covering a number of the hot-button topics about which humanists care deeply. You may find it worthwhile to read these, see how they flow from the uniquely humanist understanding of the world, and reflect upon how that translates to our own lives and positions, which likely match up with remarkable accuracy. Chapter Nine looks at how we live our humanism, from the meaning of life and the joys we find in it to death and thoughts about immortality. Chapter Ten looks squarely at social activism, pointing out best practices for activism, charitable giving, and charitable work like addiction recovery, as well as other ways to make change. The final chapter considers why conclusions aren't enough, and how an applied humanism is essential if we are truly interested in bringing about the positive change we envision.

Resources follow, including a glossary of nontheist movement related terms you may want to peruse, perhaps even in advance.

Please let me know your thoughts about what you read and the ideas that the topics may generate. I travel extensively throughout the nation, and one of the perks for me is getting the chance to learn so much about humanists I meet and to hear their creative suggestions for bettering our efforts to improve the world little by little. In fact, through such communications with me and other leaders of the humanist movement, individual humanists have a very real access to contributing to the direction of humanism itself.

Contact me at creatingchange@americanhumanist.org and follow me on Facebook and Twitter.

PART I

FOUNDATIONS

"Why is humanism not the preeminent belief of humankind?"

– Joyce Carol Oates, in her acceptance speech for
the 2007 Humanist of the Year Award

CHAPTER 1

Is Humanism Right for Me?

In order to create meaningful and long-lasting positive change, it won't do to act without firm philosophical grounding, just as it's not enough to subscribe to any starry-eyed theory that doesn't actually work in practice. To arrive at a lifestance that can truly be an instigator of better lives for ourselves and our society, we need to take an interdisciplinary approach that integrates all we know about science, history, relationships, and the nature of the universe. And unlike purveyors of traditional religion, we need to constantly evolve our thinking based on our rapidly increasing knowledge.

What does it mean to be a humanist?

Humanism isn't a religion in the traditional sense as there are no unchanging rules, no set of beliefs one must follow, no higher power one must give over to, and no requirement to attend services or pray at bedtime. It's not just a philosophy in the common sense as it informs beyond the boundaries of the pursuit of knowledge and wisdom into aesthetics and daily living. It's not a political dogma because it doesn't dictate a specific platform of unchanging positions. Some call it a worldview or lifestance because it's intended to address all the realms traditionally associated with philosophy, religion, and simply living a good life.

Humanism is the not so radical idea that you can be good without a belief in a god. It's the discovery that you not only don't need outdated texts or god experts to make good choices, but that those are frequently poor resources for decision making. Humanists affirm our ability and responsibility to lead ethical lives of personal fulfillment that aspire to the greater good of humanity. We ground that pursuit, not in theism or other supernatural beliefs, but in the best of modern knowledge determined from trial and error and the scientific process.

And that's exactly what the early leaders of the modern humanist movement had in mind as they laid the groundwork for the movement in the first part of the twentieth century. These scholars and leaders came to understand that the world does not depend on any god intervening in our daily lives and that much of what they were taught about the validity of ancient texts and divine revelations was simply false. The humanism we develop together as a community offers us a chance to develop a much sounder basis for living.

Moreover, it's worth emphasizing that humanists believe behaving well need not be motivated by some idle hope for eternal "payback." Long-time honorary president of the American Humanist Association Kurt Vonnegut, in grasping that death is the end point for all humans, put it this way: "Being a humanist means trying to behave decently without expectation of rewards or punishment after you are dead."

Humanism is a foundation for strong convictions. With a basis that includes scientific reasoning, compassion born of empathy, and an egalitarian sense of justice for the rights of minorities, humanism is a forward-looking, reality based worldview.

The first pillar is the unflagging dedication to the **scientific method**, relied upon because experience has proven it reliable. For the humanist, this method for deriving answers is supreme. Believing that knowledge of the world is derived through observation, experimentation, and rational analysis automatically rules out many possible conclusions. Because of this approach, humanists reject supernatural sources, unexamined dogma, and overly simplistic—or absolutist—concepts of good and evil.

Humanists don't simply disbelieve religious explanations; rather, we find that such explanations don't stand up to reasonable scientific scrutiny. When supernatural claims of transcendence such as assertions of rebirth or divine intervention are confronted

4

with scientific review, it's not only clear that the evidence doesn't support them, but that including such religiously rooted ideas in our understanding of the world requires living with severe cognitive dissonance or undoing much of what we've learned about how the world actually works.

"Faith" itself is a word which implies trust or belief without evidence. In an admirable effort to seek common ground with religious friends, I've heard humanists speak about their faith in science, reason or humanity. But, while I may represent a minority viewpoint on this issue, I think it's not really faith that those humanists are referring to since it's a trust based in evidence and experience. Humanists understand how the world works, have plenty of reason to trust in the efficacy of science, and have a confidence in humanity based on education about the course of history. It seems to me that religious language, which may confuse instead of clarify, can always be replaced with language better describing what is really meant. Those humanists who continue to employ religious terminology might make a special effort to provide context to ensure they aren't misunderstood.

Also a pillar of humanism is **empathy**, which links science with what distinguishes humanism as a positive philosophy. Empathy is the capacity to recognize and share feelings experienced by others. Our human history of slowly moving away from violence can be explained in part by this virtue, for as people came to know each other better with the advent of cities, transportation opportunities, and online communications, we empathetically realized that we all strive to avoid suffering and seek happiness—not only for ourselves, but for others as well. We all need a certain amount of empathy to feel compassion for others and to understand that we are all humans.

It's through the cultivation of empathy that we develop a deep-seated **compassion** for humankind and the world at large. In situations where we have the courage to act compassionately, instigating such action is a natural result, both logically and emotionally, from strong feelings of empathy. As Stephen Post found in *Altruism, Happiness, and Health: It's Good to Be Good*, benefiting society maximizes individual happiness and raises the potential of humanity. Indeed, a primary purpose of engaging the scientific method is to pursue compassionate goals, to improve the world through the quest for knowledge, and to use that knowledge to benefit ourselves and society. Since we don't assume the validity of ancient books or those who profess to communicate with higher powers, only reason, observation, experience, and action provide reliable, time-tested tools for realizing compassionate ends.

Given this focus on reason and compassion, humanists are driven to embrace social policies that are inclusive, diffuse political power, and foster self-determination. This is the source of our embrace of democracy as well as individual, social, and human rights.

Such a commitment to compassion might only have modest effects on our positions were it not for the accompanying commitment to an **egalitarian-based sense of fairness**, the third pillar of humanism. Compassion without egalitarianism is hollow. Such compassion is reminiscent of the compassion of ancient Hindu societies, which undid any interest they had in compassion by stratifying society into castes that allowed many to be considered less than human. Similarly, a number of pre-Civil War Christian leaders urged slave owners to be kind to their slaves, but such "compassion" was worthless within the confines of slavery. And when conservative Christians or Muslims say the husband should be the head of the household, but use his power kindly, they fool themselves if they think of this as meaningful compassion.

This principle of egalitarianism is the conviction that humans are basically equal despite differences in aptitude, and that each person should be treated as having inherent worth. Given such humanist reasoning, there's plenty of room for differing outcomes based on intellect, ability, creativity and hard work. But acceptance of inequality between ethnic, cultural or other groups as grounds for discrimination against them is insupportable. This leads us to the conclusion that we live on this one world as one people. Politically, it discourages chauvinistic nationalism and supports international cooperation.

Despite the problems of religion **humanism is marked by its positive approach.**

Nearly every humanist holds some anti-religious notions, as there is much wrong and even scarily dangerous about traditional religion. Psychologist Stephen Uhl, a former priest, explains: "A necessary stance of supernatural religions is that one's faith must override or control one's reason; for the believer, logic is secondary to faith. This subjecting of humankind's highest natural power to faith can lead to various sorts of illogical and destructive results: inter-faith terrorism, overpopulation, repression of free scientific inquiry, impoverishing the poor and ignorant contributors to dubious causes, to name a few. But I think the most destructive result of subjecting reason to faith is the loss of respect for our highest power, the logical human mind with its ability to problem-solve responsibly." Given religion's dubious past and present, it would be surprising if anyone, religious or not, didn't harbor some reservations about the institution.

And many humanists may experience anti-theistic periods in their life when they feel that countering the harm of religion is their best overall emphasis. But that essentially negative mindset isn't what characterizes the thrust of humanist aspirations.

After all, it's tiresome to always talk about what we don't believe. A consistently negative approach is simply unhealthy and less productive than alternatives. Instead of always wrestling with issues that insult our integrity and allowing others to determine the terms of the debate, we approach questions in more productive ways. For instance:

- Rather than asking: Do you accept the supreme authority of a book or institution?
  We ask: Do you explore science, literature, and art with an open mind?

- Rather than asking: Do you give exclusive allegiance to a unique prophet or savior?
  We ask: Do you value your own experience and worth?

- Rather than asking: Do you believe in an absolute, a personal god, an immortal soul?
  We ask: Do you act for the good of humanity, including future generations?
- Rather than asking: Do you trust in an external purpose guiding the universe?
  We ask: Do you create your own meanings and purposes?

Humanists are inherently skeptical of traditional religion, but neither is traditional religion ignored, for no fount of ideas should be set aside without consideration. For instance, Tibetan Buddhist Pema Chödrön instructs us to "Start where you are." This means that we can't explain what we do not yet understand, and it's acceptable to live in a world that still has mysteries. However, it also means that we do what we can to uncover those mysteries, and, looking at the course of history, we have every reason to believe that, more and more over time, we will steadily shed light on what we do not yet know. Starting where you are also means not disregarding what has been learned. Just as mathematicians and psychologists study the knowledge that their disciplines have accumulated and seek to build upon them, humanists do the same instead of constantly trying to reinvent the wheel. Respecting the wisdom of experts in their fields doesn't mean that we just dogmatically stand by what's been said. We learn from experts and creatives alike, questioning everything, while accepting the parts with reasonable proof that fit together with what we know of the world and most simply explain what remains.

Humanists don't have a hierarchy with a leader as Catholics do in their pope, calling the shots for what is and what isn't humanism. The best we can do is to bring together a coalition of those who feel common agreement can be found. The International Humanist and Ethical Union, the international association and lobbying arm for a hundred national groups, defines humanism as "a democratic and ethical lifestance that affirms that human beings have the right and responsibility to give meaning and shape to their own lives. Humanism stands for the building of a more humane society through an ethics based on human and other natural values in a spirit of reason and free inquiry through human capabilities. Humanism is not theistic and it does not accept supernatural views of reality." That definition captures much of humanism, but for a shorter treatment, the American Humanist Association emblazons on its logo that humanists are "Good Without a God."

Humanists resonate with particular viewpoints that disdain accepting any philosophy or ideology whole cloth, so please don't be dissuaded if you find a few points of disagreement. But if much of the above fits with your understanding of the world, you're probably in the right place.

CHAPTER 2

Identifying and Coming Out

Part of deciding whether or not you're in the right place is hearing the journeys people took to get here. While an increasing number of people are being raised in a humanistic manner, such folks still represent a minority of active humanists today. For the rest of us, seeing how others followed a similar path of falling away from a former faith that increasingly didn't make sense to them is a good way to affirm one's own experience. Fortunately, once we know we're in a safe space, humanists are frequently eager to share our stories about how we came to appreciate the humanist identity. I've found this to be especially true when it involves a transition from a faith-based perspective.

But taking a path divergent from the traditional god belief is not one widely accepted in the United States today, so it's not surprising that this is frequently a struggle. In fact, even when the theistic divide is permanently crossed, the decision to be public about one's humanist identity is also a tough one.

For me, like many I've met who come from theistic backgrounds, my journey to a new way of thinking was part of a lifelong effort to discard myths and seek truths—truths with a lower case "t" that realize the value of critical inquiry. Raised Catholic in upstate New York, I didn't accept the church's teachings for too long, as I didn't think the all-good, all-powerful God made very much sense in the real world we all live in.

By the age of eleven, while in my Sunday CCD class (which I probably never knew stood for Confraternity of Christian Doctrine), I got it into my head to ask the priest who was visiting the classroom a classical question. "Father Keaveney," I said, "if God is all-good, why is there a hell?" He told me how God's gift of free will would not be complete unless we could choose to do good or evil. I didn't quite understand how it could be a good thing for us to have the choice to choose evil, or why anyone would make such a choice freely, but I suppressed my doubt for a time, figuring it was my inability to comprehend the mysteries of faith.

IELPING THE STATUE OF LIBERTY...Fifth graders [left to right] 'racy Strang, Diane Nicolini, Lori Porcelli and Roy Speckhardt lisplay bottles and cans they have collected to raise funds for repair f the Statue of Liberty. The students at George Fischer Middle chool in Carmel donned Statue of Liberty grab for their special ollection. COURIER Photo by EGO

PHOTO COURTESY PUTNAM COUNTY *COURIER*

Later that school year I got sent to the principal by my home-room teacher for not saying the Pledge of Allegiance. It wasn't that I no longer believed in God, nor was I feeling unpatriotic, but I found something wrong with seeing my teacher in the position of leading the class in a pledge that referred to faith in God. The assistant principal, Mr. Perri, a good-hearted big man who probably just wanted to avoid trouble, tempted me out of my protest by suggesting that I at least stand for the Pledge and say it for the sake of not causing trouble. Feeling the pressure to conform, and recognizing that everyone involved was well-meaning, I caved. My homeroom teacher, Ms. Berger, was not a religious conservative; in fact, she was a Jewish Holocaust survivor and a progressive. So while I did go back to saying the Pledge, that instance was the last time I agreed to play along and keep my convictions to myself.

A couple of years later I remember my European history teacher, Mr. Corini, going off on a tangent, as he sometimes did, describing in detail some of the interesting and funny things that were done by and to Catholic popes in the Middle Ages. A fellow student of mine, Peggy Looney, objected, saying she was interested in possibly studying to be a nun and believed he was being sacrilegious. Mr. Corini responded by telling the class how he would not suggest studying religion or theology too closely because it might cause you to lose faith and that you might be happier if you remained faithful. Knowing he was a graduate of seminary, it wasn't too hard to tell that he was basically saying that religion cannot withstand the scrutiny of reason. My teacher realized he said too much and quickly changed the subject, but I couldn't help but consider his words, as well as what it was that made him reticent to speak about it further.

It was in college where I realized I was an atheist. And for a while I suppose I was an anti-theist too, because as soon as I stepped away from religious faith, all its evils seemed worse than ever. It took me some time to regain respect for religious thinkers and faithful humanitarians, but it was in that process that I opened myself to the more positive light of humanism.

It was another big step for me when I learned in my Western Civilization class in my first year of college that many of the stories in the Old Testament are slightly different versions of much older stories from ancient Mesopotamia, stories the Mesopotamians apparently considered to be myths. It seemed hard to believe that anyone could stand by the accuracy of stories whose first tellers were unashamed to say that they made them up. And when I took Philosophy 101, I gained the knowledge and the methodology to study my beliefs and where they came from. It was then that I finally lost my theism, but I wasn't yet ready for humanism because I was too angry to be a positive-minded humanist. "Why don't my family, friends, community, and society see through the myth of religion?" I thought.

During my undergraduate studies at Mary Washington College, I took courses coincidentally taught by humanists from a variety of backgrounds, the most prominent of which was civil rights leader James Farmer. The sociology courses I took covered many social problems driven by ignorance: racism, sexism, ageism, homophobia, and classism. The recognition of the many deep-seated myths our society clings to, along with a glimpse into the harm that they can cause, inspired me to choose a career focusing on dispelling these myths and righting the resulting wrongs.

I find myself driven by the desire to add my humanist voice to advocate for the use of scientific methods for ascertaining truths we can act upon, as well as prompt others to root their own goals and ideals in a firm foundation that's both compassionate and egalitarian. And even though I didn't recognize it at first, these aims represent the very pillars of humanism.

While I had heard about humanism in college, I didn't connect it to my nontheistic search for knowledge and wisdom. Believing I was among the few who thought as I did, I started a website in 1995, Progressivism.org, where I tried to outline my thinking. But after running into humanism at every turn of my research, I "caved" and joined the American Humanist Association—after all, they did promise me a free book explaining what it was about: Corliss Lamont's *The Philosophy of Humanism*. I immediately saw that I was recreating the wheel and stopped my side philosophy business. I saw how humanism was uniquely open to an evolutionary form of philosophy, how humanism includes positions on life and politics that perfectly meshed with my own, and how humanism was a lifestance that can truly resonate with modern life—so even though humanist publications seemed a little stodgy at the time, I appreciated the openness to change as an opportunity to make a difference.

As I strove to challenge the Religious Right as well as sexism, racism and homophobia, I found religious allies at every turn. These folks weren't so unenlightened as I presumed in college but were just as eager to do good as I was. So I ended up working for a number of years for the Interfaith Alliance, a pro-church-state separation organization that spends much of its time fighting fundamentalism.

I recall one day participating in a strategic planning session at the Interfaith Alliance where we were trying to drill down to why we all wanted to do good and how we decided what was right and just. Some of them pointed to holy books, but when asked why they interpreted them the way they did, instead of in a more conservative way, they were hard-pressed to answer. I left that meeting realizing that regardless of their faith traditions and regardless of whether or not they noticed it, these freethinking folks were acting on humanist foundations. Sure, some had to really mentally rearrange what their holy books were telling them to get to that point, but they did that rearranging because they shared our core humanist understandings of the world.

After several years at the Interfaith Alliance, receiving my MBA in the meantime, and becoming more and more committed to raising public awareness of nontheists like me, I saw an opportunity to put my humanist ideals directly to work when I joined the American Humanist Association staff in 2001. It was an "Aha!" moment in many ways. Not only did I say, "Aha! Here's the philosophy I've been searching for!" but I also said, "Aha! Here's the political organization I've been searching for." And yet another "Aha! Here's the way to accomplish long-lasting progressive change since the AHA doesn't just tackle one issue at a time." Through humanism, the American Humanist Association provides an alternative worldview that inspires people to change the way they look at the world, harness a secular perspective bolstered by compassion, and act in ways to better society.

For American Humanist Association board member, author, and professor Dr. Anthony Pinn, his transformation was a more dramatic one than mine. Tony was raised in a profoundly religious environment in Buffalo, New York. With his devout mother providing the biggest early influence and the local minister tapping him for a career in the pulpit, Tony became a rising star in his local African Methodist Episcopal church. Preaching his first sermon by age twelve and becoming ordained in an evangelical ministry by eighteen, humanism wasn't an available option. In fact, Tony's religion was a "speaking-in-tongues" kind of faith where one was expected to be regularly moved by a direct connection to the Holy Spirit in a God-fearing way. This faith seemed firmly intact as he spent time in white fundamentalist West Seneca Christian School and then began college at Columbia University. While in New York, Tony spent time ministering at the influential Bridge Street AME Church, the oldest continuing African American congregation in Brooklyn. With Christian faith permeating much of his life, and himself on the doorstep of a life of distinction in the church, his intellectual curiosity had to have been remarkably strong for him to walk down the roads that lead to atheism and humanism.

Tony's intellectual inquisitiveness, along with New York City and Columbia University's atmosphere of skeptical exploration, was the combination that opened doors to knowledge that conflicted with the Christian story. This newly discovered knowledge suggested the possibility of better answers to the social problems communities grapple with than that which religion provided. Upon discovering historical and philosophical truths that didn't fit with a biblical view, Tony began to modify his faith gradually away from the literal Bible and the evangelical position of revealed truth. Over time he came to see the conclusions reached through academia and the church as less and less compatible.

It was with such seeds of doubt firmly planted that Tony went on to Harvard Divinity School, where they blossomed into a more and more pragmatic approach that embraced realism. Harvard was a place where the Bible didn't take precedence over science and reason. At the same time, Tony came to better appreciate the pluralism within African American faith communities and saw value in remaining a part of that world. So he continued to adjust his own faith to fit with what he learned about life in and out of academic circles. Still preaching, but instead of seeking magical unison with the Holy Spirit, he focused on imparting what he'd learned about ethics and morality.

But even a liberalized belief wasn't going to survive Tony's probing analysis of theism. As he completed the Masters of Divinity program at Harvard and went on to the PhD program, he realized that the more he asked himself where he could find God's presence affecting the world, the more it became clear that such an effect simply wasn't there. Tony finally concluded, as he explained in his book, *Writing God's Obituary*, that "God never existed but has always been nothing more than a symbol, a piece of language and culture constructed by humans."

Many atheists and agnostics I've met, especially those from religious households, went through (or may still be going through) a time of anger at the religious for their tenacious attachment to a belief system with no evidence and their willingness to inculcate others in something so unsupported. But that conclusion for Tony was such a natural next step in the steady progression of his views that it was accompanied by neither a jarring change nor a period of anger over having been misled. "I did not feel lost as a consequence of this decision, and I didn't feel like I'd lost anything substantive," Tony remarked.

After earning his PhD at Harvard, Tony went on to teach first at Macalester College in St Paul. His atheism wasn't a secret, and his research and dissertation helped him explore how humanism was an important aspect of African American thought. When his dissertation was published as a book, it first provided a focal point for having this conversation in broader academic circles. But the conversation suddenly became host to a larger audience when the *Minneapolis Star Tribune* ran a story on his arguments and highlighted his atheism.

The article generated numerous letters and calls condemning his lack of belief in God, and suggesting that as an atheist, he shouldn't be allowed to teach in the religion department. Such criticisms revealed the prejudice against atheists since no one was questioning whether or not professors of one religion can teach about another. Religious parents don't typically have anywhere near the same concern about their children converting from one religion to another, as long as they don't become atheists.

While the college officials stood by him, Minnesotans in and out of the college were not so supportive. It became apparent that the theistic majority felt free to disrespect the sizable nontheistic minority, but that it was a break in protocol if an atheist was to express their honest view of the inadequacies of religion. If anything, this seemed magnified in the Minnesotan African American communities with which Tony was connected.

Atheists, humanists, and Unitarian Universalists in the Twin Cities reached out to Tony, inviting him to their groups and providing him a platform to speak. While he'd had some knowledge of the humanist movement before, this was the catalyst for that connection to form. Unfortunately, it also exposed the ignorance and outdated ideas regarding race issues within humanism at that time. But Tony's involvement, and that of many others, helped slowly improve the situation as did a gradual move in recent years toward a broader humanist base that naturally attracts younger and more diverse people. While there's still a struggle to shed old ways of thinking and doing for fresh approaches to diversifying the movement, progress is evident.

Today Tony continues to teach and is the Agnes Cullen Arnold Professor of Humanities and professor of religious studies at Rice University. He is the research director for the Institute for Humanist Studies and a board member of the American Humanist Association. In his work, Tony understands that different theistic traditions have an undeniable and continuing influence and cultural value in African American communities, making their continued study of significant value.

Tony "rejected God because the concept of God had no demonstrated ability to help people based on where they are and in light of the issues with which they wrestle." However, he sees humanism as having that ability and the potential to provide for the greater good. And so Tony brings this knowledge to his leadership in the humanist movement in order to help us embark on our next steps to advance humanist thought and action.

For author, psychiatrist, and psychoanalyst Dr. Janet Jeppson Asimov, becoming a humanist was as natural as a cherry tree flowering in springtime. Janet attended various Protestant Sunday schools near her home in New Rochelle, New York, because her Utah-raised, ex-Mormon parents wished to fit into that non-Mormon community. Her household was comparatively quite secular. Providing a clue to her experience, her father went to medical school instead of going on the mission expected of young men in the Mormon Church. And despite occasional pressure from extended family members, her parents didn't have her baptized, nor did she have to endure other rituals of indoctrination.

While not everyone growing up during the Great Depression and coming of age during World War II developed that humanistic ability to retain hope while accepting the full significance of our challenges, Janet did. By the age of thirteen, Janet's inquisitive mind and advanced reading comprehension led her to learn from author Lin Yutang's practical and nontheistic wisdom in *The Importance of Living*, perhaps providing a humanistic base for her ongoing intellectual development.

She began to reject supernatural beliefs even before more formal education in biblical history during her undergraduate education at Wellesley College. In her *Notes For a Memoir*, Janet wrote: "At Wellesley, I came to think of death as disorganization of the patterns called living, with nothing supernatural left over, and began to develop a working philosophy of life which I've never been able to explain very well but which suits me." This striving for one's own approach to the questions of life put Janet in good company with many humanists past and present.

After transferring from Wellesley to Stanford University, where she received her B.A., Janet went on to earn an M.D. degree from New York University Medical School and complete her residency in psychiatry at Bellevue Hospital. Continuing her education at the William Alanson White Institute of Psychoanalysis, she studied under renowned social psychologist and psychoanalyst, Erich Fromm, who was himself later honored by the American Humanist Association as Humanist of the Year in 1966.

Fromm inspired Janet to acknowledge the brevity of life and experience life to the fullest. On finding out that Janet's father and her analyst both died recently, he explained to her the human reluctance to be fully alive because of the associated necessary acceptance of inevitable change and continued to take the time to be there for her. Janet said that the experience highlighted the "power of even momentary intense human rapport and the importance of letting oneself be fully alive even when it hurts." She came to realize there aren't permanent happy endings, but happier lives are worth hoping for and working toward.

During this time she met the prolific author Isaac Asimov at the annual banquet of the Mystery Writers of America, when they both attended a presentation by Eleanor Roosevelt. She would marry Isaac in 1973 and they would go on to co-author several children's science fiction novels together. Isaac later became president of the American Humanist Association between 1985 and his death in April of 1992.

Janet fully embraces the concept of lifelong learning, as did Isaac. During lectures they attended at the American Museum of Natural History as part of that continuing education, Janet found much detail that disproved the so-called intelligent design idea that "humans are so perfect that God must have created them." She recognized that our flaws are numerous—adult humans are the only mammals whose windpipes and gullets cross, thus amplifying risk of death by choking; the human eye, part of an evolutionary chain of sensory development, has blind spots due to the ganglion cell axons exiting the eye in a suboptimal position; human sinuses are supposed to drain when we're on our hands and knees, but not when we are standing up straight; our reproductive openings are rather close and conflated with our excretory openings—and male nipples? Enough said. In response to intelligent design adherents, Janet remarked: "I feel sorry for religious people who cling to the idea that God created everything…In evolution, parts of the body are put to other uses because they are there—whereas an omniscient creator would surely be smart enough to design a better thing from scratch."

In *Notes on a Memoir*, Janet expresses that trying hard to understand ourselves is a defining characteristic of being human, even if it doesn't result in the comfort provided by unquestioning faith in a supposed omnipotent being who knows us completely. Speaking further on the matter Janet said: "Religion is one of the patterns created by human imagination to cope with those uncomfortable problems of relatedness, mortality, and meaninglessness."

So it wasn't a surprise that her wedding ceremony to Isaac, presided over by Ethical Culture Leader Edward Ericson, was completely nontheist. Janet mentioned that she thinks of Ethical Culture, like humanism and even science itself, as adding a sort of religious dimension "by celebrating reason and respect for life."

On Mormonism, Janet had some positive things to say but expressed her disappointment in their "embarrassingly tardy [1978] official recognition of racial equality, their narrow-minded Republicanism, and their really silly theology." Of course, Mormonism doesn't have a monopoly on the bad ideas. As Janet said: "It was nice that the pope has officially moved creationism back a few billion years, but I wish the church would decide that God didn't intend for *homo sap* to multiply quite so fruitfully…."

In trying to grapple with the persistence of religion, Janet pointed out its psychological connection with the childhood need for direction. She said, "In childhood, we don't understand what the parent is doing or saying, so in adulthood people recreate that parent in a god who is to be followed on faith, not rational understanding. Gods were vital to primitive cultures because, before science was invented and began to explain things, so much was not understood, and feared. Fear promotes irrational ideas." She added, "I'm not totally against religion per se, because most people seem to need a sense of being part of a consoling support system."

Having been told that rules are what held Jewish culture together, Janet, seeing that religion "tends to disconnect and divide humanity," responded: "I've decided that I disapprove of holding cultures together. Let everything change."

Perhaps best summarizing her respectful but honest assessment of religion, Janet wrote: "I can respect people able to keep their minds open while enjoying whatever conventional organized religion they need—providing they don't depend on their religious organizations to do their thinking for them."

I met Janet in New York several years ago and was immediately captivated by her unique combination of generosity, directness, and wit. It matches her honest and insightful writing. I'm pleased that Janet continues to write, including for the American Humanist Association's online magazine, *TheHumanist.com*.

These vignettes (including my own) should suggest something of the journey I spoke of at the outset of this chapter: Namely, that if humanism is a path you might wish to embark on, it may first be useful to understand how others came to select this way of life for themselves.

CHAPTER 3

An Argument for Humanism

Since you've made it this far, and you haven't indignantly tossed this book aside, you're very likely a humanist. But, if so, how did you become one? And was it for the best? Is it time now to start calling yourself a humanist?

There's considerable debate as to whether or not we are biologically predisposed toward theism—whether our natural bent is to accept extraordinary claims without evidence, or whether we may be biologically primed for skepticism. Few would argue that our religiosity is solely determined by our genes or that it's completely disconnected from them. So, in all likelihood, there's a bit of both heredity and experience involved in us being who we are today. Some feel that the predisposition toward believing what others tell them without serious analysis is an evolutionary advantage, a trait humanity acquired along the way so that children learn more quickly by tending to believe what their parents tell them. But in today's world such a predisposition might have more drawbacks than advantages.

While what we believe may change greatly over our lifespans, it appears that our tendency toward skepticism, just like our understanding of morality, is acquired at a relatively early age. As Albert Einstein said: "There is nothing divine about morality; it is a purely human affair." And a careful study of moral questions confirms this. Psychologist Jean Piaget came to understand this when he looked for morality in very young children who had not had much exposure to a complex moral system in their secular or religious education, nor did they yet have the mental equipment to understand a learned morality. When he observed the morality of their experience playing the game of marbles, Piaget found several stages of development among small children. In the first phase, marbles were simply an object children tested their motor skills on; infants tasted them, buried them, piled them up, threw them, and so on. Next, some of these behaviors became ritualized as if associated with particular thoughts of the infants performing them.

Within two years, small children old enough to speak were making some effort to imitate the rules of the game as practiced by older children. They were incapable of remembering or understanding all these rules, and each child played only against herself or himself, but they still considered the rules as highly valuable. Later, as children mastered the rules of marbles, a keen sense of fairness arose to influence subsequent creation and adaptation of the rules.

Finally, though fairness remained key, older children came to regard the rules as their collective creation, *a contract they formed to be able to play with one another.* Thus the rules evolved to define the conditions for cooperation, the penalties for defection, and how rules might be amended or replaced. This research nicely shows how humans are rule-creating animals that start developing individualized moralities in early childhood.

More recent studies of even younger children (babies really) have not only confirmed but also extended Piaget's work. In the American Psychological Association's *Science Watch*, Kirsten Weir reports research evidencing that babies under two (long before exposure to religion) can distinguish between good and bad people, have an intrinsic desire to be helpful, comprehend basic equality-based fairness, and understand that you must earn your fair share. Weir attributes growth in moral behavior to cognitive development rather than to learned rules from sources like religion. This development in infancy shows why children aged seven or eight realize that fairness is a priority, even in situations where they would otherwise get the upper hand.

The concept of the golden rule, expanded to empathetically take others' perspectives into consideration—do unto others as they would want done unto them—is repeated in variations throughout most religions and cultures. While it doesn't provide a sole guide to action, and it may be harder to carry out than it sounds, it frames our thinking about all others in the light of our own wants and desires, pains and trials, and joys and happy experiences. Kids get this concept at an early age even if it may take a lifetime for them to perfect it.

I've talked with many humanists who expressed doubts at an early age, not just about the faith they'd been introduced to, but other authority-given information as well. While it's not universal and doesn't always lead to a fast track to humanism, humanists appear to have a tendency toward investigating truths for themselves. Seeming exceptions to this rule of inherent skepticism include those who experience a moment of fresh understanding, often after a crisis in life, or break with their previously prevailing religious perspective. I've even talked to a number of former ministers who fit this bill.

And of course, there are a growing number of people who have been or are being raised in a nontheist tradition. From Unitarian Universalist, to Ethical Culturists, to families that choose to opt out of the religion business, there are millions of people who never were sold the idea that you should believe in something that contradicts the evidence.

It turns out that nonreligious kids are more mild and generous than religious ones as well. A 2015 study, called The Negative Association between Religiousness and Children's Altruism across the World confirmed this to be accurate.

Is Humanism Radical?

"There may not be one Truth—there may be several truths—but saying that is not to say that reality doesn't exist."
– Margaret Atwood, in a 1997 *Mother Jones* interview

Now that you've opened the door to an exploration of humanism, is humanism an idea widely embraced, or inherently having the potential to be? Philosopher Paul Kurtz affirmed that the goal of humanistic morality "is the enhancement of the good life: happiness and well-being for the widest number of individuals," and that this goal is not limited to our humanist minority: "This point of view came into prominence [in Europe] during the Renaissance; it is expressed in the Declaration of Independence, and indeed in virtually every modern democratic system of ethics. People may dispute about the meaning of happiness and well-being, but nonetheless most humanists say that the good life involves satisfying and pleasurable experience, creative actualization, and human realization."

Both religious and nonreligious people can share this goal. To reject it would be to repeal the modern world. Indeed, while there is a minority in this country composed of religious fundamentalists who try to paint humanism as far outside the mainstream, our core values are the very essence of humanity and are not extreme in any way.

Like most modern people of any religion or philosophy do in at least parts of their lives, we seek our knowledge from analysis of the observable world for our decision making. It's not just lengthy research we do ourselves or relegate to experts, but incorporated in our ordinary life when making daily decisions about what would be healthy for us to buy at the grocery store or what weekend activities we might plan that we'd enjoy the most. These are among the many ways we use reason and to some extent, the scientific process, in everyday life, demonstrating that science is a regular part of modern living.

As Unitarian Universalist Association President Peter Morales wrote in his *New Atlantis* journal article "Science and the Search for Meaning" "science is based on a radically democratic way of knowing, in the sense that scientific truth is comprised of the things we can all experience—not on private experiences, accessible only to putatively gifted individuals." Morales accurately points out that science is a process for obtaining information where any person has a chance to change everyone's minds if they can prove their point. There's no faith required to accept what we've learned from science as being the best answers currently available. Or, as Neil DeGrasse Tyson simply says, "Science is true whether you believe in it or not!"

This isn't really radical at all. What would be radical would be accepting knowledge obtained by any other means.

Unfortunately, in the same article, Morales makes the mistake of trying to carve out part of our world and suggest it's somehow outside the laws that explain everything else. He writes that "questions about meaning are not scientific questions" and goes on to relegate such questions to the realm of religion, as if untouched by science. But this tendency of creating a safe space for religion tucked away from the rigors of science, so as to avoid being disproved, is at least an oversight. In truth, we can and do use the same scientifically-rigorous approaches of observation, analysis, trial and error, and conclusion when approaching questions of meaning and purpose.

For many, the idea of approaching moral and meaning-type questions scientifically brings to mind scientists in lab coats measuring chemicals, firing up Bunsen burners, or analyzing brain tissues. This natural bias toward viewing science in a narrow laboratory context helps explain why even people, including Nobel Laureate and 2002 AHA Humanist of the Year Steven Weinberg, said there can't be a humanist, science-consistent morality. Weinberg suggests that science just doesn't have the tools to measure such phenomena. But this sort of preconceived notion overlooks what we all know about the scientific method and the nature of scientific reasoning that flows from it.

Science isn't confined to the ivory tower and research institutions; it is a basic method for gaining improved understandings. When my youngest daughter Riley once sat in her high chair, took some of her food, and tossed it on the ground to see what happened, that was practicing science. It's really a process for asking tough questions and looking at possible answers through the lens of reality. It's applicable to any natural phenomenon including morality and meaning. When viewed with the most sophisticated powers of our scientific reasoning, our drive to help humanity is a sensible one and our reliance on empathy is a recognizable good.

By accepting the scientific process as the best method for determining all types of knowledge, we have the opportunity to build humanity's knowledge base in a deliberate and positive manner. Through the science of human psychology we have a viable way of empirically ascertaining how happiness is linked to the humanistic values that are woven into our very nature. And furthermore, by recognizing that our skepticism and morality are human inventions within our control, we can build upon our foundations and better ourselves and our communities.

In developing our moralities, we can examine our own maxims, really think about what they mean, and find positive ways to integrate our rules for living into our daily lives. As Unitarian Universalist minister Kendyl Gibbons said: "If there is no personality governing the universe and promising us love, justice, and meaning on some ontological bottom line, then it is all the more necessary for us, flawed and finite as we are, to give love, to enact justice, and to build meaning here and now."

With nothing stopping us from truly learning from history and the trial and error of the present, we can apply what we've learned immediately, discarding outdated ideas and practices and replacing them with behaviors that help all of us live the good life.

Crossing the Theistic Divide

With books like Richard Dawkins' *The God Delusion*, Christopher Hitchens' *God is Not Great*, and Reginald Exton's *Make the Break (If You Can)*, there's no need to be redundant here, explaining how theism no longer makes sense in the modern world. But it's still worth a brief consideration since getting to that conclusion is often a misunderstood process.

Comedian George Carlin said: "I've begun worshipping the sun for a number of reasons. First of all, unlike some other gods I could mention, I can see the sun. It's there for me every day. And the things it brings me are quite apparent all the time: heat, light, food, and a lovely day. There's no mystery, no one asks for money, I don't have to dress up, and there's no boring pageantry. And interestingly enough, I have found that the prayers I offer to the sun and the prayers I formerly offered to 'God' are all answered at about the same fifty percent rate."

Leaving theism—a belief system based on a god or gods—can mean many different things to different people. I'm convinced that the truly substantive break is the one that results in accepting that there is no divine personality or supernatural force in control of the day-to-day events in our lives. When we come into money or lose a job, when our land experiences floods or droughts, when our country finds peace or enters wars, there are this-worldly reasons for these events. Appealing to a mystical force will do no good.

In fact, prayer may even do harm. According to the 2006 Study of the Therapeutic Effects of Intercessory Prayer (STEP), not only did prayer not result in improved mortality rates for cardiac bypass patients, but those who were aware they were being prayed for fared slightly worse, perhaps because of the anxiety they felt in feeling pressure to recover.

Since a foundational principle of humanism is that we base our knowledge on reason and don't rely on faith, belief in an intervening higher power isn't compatible with humanism.

Beyond that, it's not really very relevant to one's decision making whether or not one goes further and says there is not now, nor was there ever any god or higher power. Unless we're cosmologists, there's not a practical difference in how a deist (one who believes in a creator god that jumpstarted the universe and stepped back from action) and an atheist makes decisions. The conclusion about the existence of gods and the label chosen to represent oneself will certainly impact public perceptions, but the practical implications are the same for atheists, agnostics, and deists.

The American Humanist Association requires no loyalty oaths or statements of belief (or lack thereof) to be a member. You don't have to be an atheist to be a humanist, even though most humanists are atheists by definition. According to most dictionaries as well as the roots of the word, atheist really means only that one doesn't have a belief system based on a god or gods; they may hold to other convictions, but to find out we'd need to know more about them than just the label *atheist*. Some people incorrectly believe that atheism implies a certainty about there being no gods—one of a number of issues some atheists like to debate.

When we conducted a rigorous survey of the AHA membership a few years back, reaching over a thousand respondents, we learned that ninety percent of our members are ninety percent sure that there isn't a god. More than two-thirds identified as atheist as well as humanist. About ten percent considered themselves agnostics. A small number of members called themselves deists, and a smaller still identified as theists, but among that last category, representing just two percent, most had their own definition for the divine that included everything (pantheism) or just themselves (autotheism). It's clear that members of the AHA don't think there's a personified being making decisions about what happens here on earth.

Uh Oh, I Think I'm Becoming an Atheist!

How does one get to being an atheist anyway? Perhaps you have been asked regularly why you no longer accept the faith you were born into. Historically, there have been numerous arguments for belief in a god, and whether or not this decision is well behind us, it's good to know about these arguments and be prepared to discuss them. Thomas Aquinas' concept of a first mover god being necessary to start the chain of causation conveniently overlooked the fact that such logic requires his god to have a cause as well. People who are convinced by their wishful thinking that individual prayers were answered don't know how improbable it would be for no coincidences like that to ever occur in their lives. And the suggestion that a beautiful and orderly world needs an intelligent designer, namely a god, does not acknowledge the ugliness and disorder in the world, nor does it bother to address the science that elegantly explains all we see in nature. These arguments for intelligent design all stall-out when we carefully review them.

Deciding there isn't a higher power governing our daily lives wasn't a long, drawn-out process for me, and this is increasingly the case for young people who see no special reason to believe in something evidence doesn't support.

For me, the decision was a puzzle with just two pieces.

The first piece is that the religious stories I was taught are full of holes and contradictions. Volumes have been written on these. Forget the contradictions about whether God is a god of war or a god of peace, whether Jesus is equal or lesser than God the Father, and what the order of creation really was. Forget the quirky errors, like the mentions that rabbits are supposed to chew their cud and snakes eat dirt. Forget the improbable miracles, like turning water into wine or blood and the environmental travesty that might ensue. For me, the real eye-opener was discovering that many Bible stories originated in pagan traditions.

If Christians say the ancient pagan traditions are myths, how does that square with the historical evidence that "the exact phrases in the Old Testament are taken from previously existing myths," as philanthropist Todd Stiefel describes in his account of why he's not a Catholic. Stiefel explained how there is "no extra-biblical evidence for the Jewish enslavement in Egypt or the Exodus" and that "the Jewish Yahweh was closely associated with El, the king of the Ugarit pantheon...El ruled over a court of less powerful deities in just the way Psalm 82 speaks of Yahweh ruling over an assembly of lesser gods." Then there's the Babylonian flood myth and the Egyptian practice of circumcision which also predate the Bible.

Invalidating very significant portions of the Bible leaves little reason to continue to believe in Christianity. The same sort of process can be explained for other faiths now that we've come to know more about ancient history and the way religions are born.

That brings us to the second piece of the puzzle, a rather easy puzzle to solve in retrospect. As much as we know that existing religions don't make sense, the second piece is the utter lack of evidence for anything transcending the world as we know it.

You'd think that in an age like ours, if there were supernatural activity really happening, it would be well-documented and replicable by now. After all, we live in a world where everyone can access detailed maps of the world through Google Earth. It's only been hundreds of years since Michael Servetus was burned at the stake for describing how blood circulates through the lungs, but we've now mapped the three billion pairs of genetic instructions in the human genome. If something (like a "soul") left the body at death, we'd know it. If there was a realm above the clouds in Earth's atmosphere, we'd see it. And if prayer worked, we'd have the proof.

The truth is not only does nothing leave the body at death, but we've studied the brain enough to understand that near-death experiences really are related to the brain's natural response to lack of oxygen. And there's a stunning lack of evidence for heaven or hell, an existence in the clouds or down below. The studies with the best methodology on prayer show that it has absolutely no impact on life outcomes (unless people know they are being prayed for, and in that case, the results are slightly negative).

So with the puzzle complete, we see that the stated extraordinary claims that religion makes are false and that the evidence indicates there are no supernatural forces at work in the universe.

Until recently Stephen Hawking was hesitant to use the words "I'm an atheist" but he finally did so in order to be clear about where he was coming from. And he elaborated in an elucidating way, saying, "In my opinion, there is no aspect of reality beyond the reach of the human mind."

After grasping all that, it's hard not to step over the theistic divide. And if you need encouragement, just look at the benefits accrued by choosing this path, such as finding a new community that connects solely on the basis of our shared humanity. According to a study completed in 2014 in *Social Indicators Research* that compares nontheist communities with religious communities, the prosocial behavior (such as community support and generosity) commonly associated with religious belief in God is actually correlated with community involvement. Both believing communities and nonbelieving communities benefit people about the same and, in non-believing communities, generosity is less likely to be parochially limited to one's in-group.

And there are better outcomes for kids as well. According to a study in *Cognitive Science*, children who don't get bombarded with religious mythology are actually better able to distinguish fact from fiction. Researchers found the religious approach resulted in "a natural credulity toward extraordinary beings with superhuman powers." It's nice to see this intuitive realization borne out in a replicable study. Telling kids facts helps them better understand the world.

Once that theistic divide is crossed, the choice of atheist, agnostic, or something even more nuanced, is one on which humanist types can spend considerable time. But no matter what choice is made, we all share much in common since we all recognize that prayer isn't a means to an end and preachers aren't speaking for a higher power, despite their rationales.

All this said, for some the break with traditional theism is a challenging one. We should give people experiencing this internal struggle a chance to explore and decide for themselves—not rush them to reach a particular conclusion.

So Many Identities

As any movement expands and incorporates the views of newcomers, members are likely to diversify. Such expansion among those who reject ancient texts and divinely revealed truth as sources of knowledge has led to people identifying in many ways while still seeing themselves as part of the nontheist movement. They use labels such as humanist, atheist, agnostic, deist, nonbeliever, nonreligious, freethinker, bright, nontheist, skeptic, secular, and more.

There are even millions of Americans who retain labels from traditional faith traditions, such as Catholic, Jewish or Buddhist, but who don't believe in an intervening god—as first clearly revealed in the Pew Religious Landscape Survey. This survey was groundbreaking since previous large-scale religious polls failed to acknowledge the millions of godless people who remain active in religions. This discovery led the American Humanist Association to launch its Paths to Humanism project (described more in the next chapter) to invite those same nontheistic religious individuals to add humanist as an additional identification.

Q.32 Which comes closest to your view of God? God is a person with whom people can have a relationship or God is an impersonal force?

| | ----Yes, believe in God or a universal spirit--- | | | | Don't believe in God | Other/ DK (VOL) | Total |
	Personal God	Impersonal force	Other/ Both/ Neither	DK/ Refused			
Total	60	25	4	3	5	3	100
Evangelical churches	79	13	4	3	0	1	100
Mainline churches	62	26	4	4	1	2	100
Historically Black churches	71	19	5	3	0	1	100
Catholic	60	29	4	4	1	2	100
Mormon	91	6	1	1	0	0	100
Orthodox	49	34	6	6	4	1	100
Jehovah's Witness	82	11	4	1	0	2	100
Other Christian	50	34	11	2	1	2	100
Jewish	25	50	4	4	10	7	100
Muslim	41	42	7	3	5	2	100
Buddhist	20	45	7	3	19	6	100
Hindu	31	53	5	2	5	3	100
Other Faiths	29	41	9	3	9	9	100
Unaffiliated	28	35	3	3	22	8	100

PEW FORUM ON RELIGION & PUBLIC LIFE / U.S. RELIGIOUS LANDSCAPE SURVEY

Our movement is made up of all those who are good without a god in their own way, not just self-identified atheists. If we were to limit the movement to only those who are willing to identify solely as atheists, the nontheist movement would look small indeed. What's more, that smallness would make it harder to achieve our shared aim of equality for all who are good without a god.

But as much as it shouldn't be required for people to give up their other identities and claim only atheism, people should still aim to be open about their not believing in a god or the supernatural. That openness makes it easier for the next nonbeliever to come out. And remaining silent won't make the problem of prejudice against us go away. In fact, in addition to the persuasive nature of coming out, which I discussed earlier, by having significant numbers in the closet, it makes our demographic look smaller in numbers than it actually is, making it harder for the community to fight for equal representation.

Those who pretend to be theistic may be acting unethically by misleading others about their beliefs. How can being closeted about one aspect of one's core worldview be unethical? It's more than just missing the opportunity to do good and compromising one's personal integrity. Hiding one's nontheism from believers actually dishonors them by underplaying the importance of their belief. Even if your non-god-belief just isn't that important to you, it's undeniably of vital importance to many people in our society with whom you communicate. Despite the rising numbers of nonbelievers, belief in a god is more than a majority idea in America. In fact, seventy-eight percent of Americans say they believe in a Christian God, and thirty-one percent believe so strongly that they interpret their Bible as the literal word of God. Not believing in a god may not be the dominant issue in your personal life (most humanists understandably have a much more positive agenda than that), but it has to be recognized that it is meaningful to others. If people are to be respected, they deserve to know who we truly are.

According to David Silverman, president of American Atheists, "Hiding your identity means lying to everyone you know, forcing them to love someone fictional out of fear that they might not like the real you. However, given the chance, most family members love the person, not the lie, and everyone benefits from a more honest relationship."

Considering the shared aim among nonbelievers to doggedly pursue the truth regarding humanity, the nature of the universe, and everything in it, there is understandably a high ethical standard for humanists and other nontheists to which we hold ourselves. There's a reason Americans swear to uphold the truth, the whole truth, and nothing but the truth. And failing to uphold the whole truth (when what's withheld matters) is a failing we should strive to overcome.

Closeted nonbelievers once showed bravery in putting aside the comforting religious stories about existence in favor of a scientific understanding of the universe and our seemingly minor role in it. If they can tap into their reservoirs of bravery once more to fight the silence regarding their nonbelief, they'll no longer have to jump through intellectual hoops and conceal themselves from those who they care about.

Of course, when people take the plunge it helps to use words that communicate clearly who they are and what they stand for. For those who know, or take the time to learn what words like humanist, skeptic, and freethinker really mean, such identifiers can actually convey considerably more than the atheist identity.

By definition, identifying as atheist indicates that one doesn't have a belief system that includes a god, nothing more. It doesn't encompass all the views that a person has when it comes to personal values, which is why terms like "humanist" and "secular" are so important. For example, secular Jews might not believe in a god but still base their ethics, or culture, on elements of Judaism that they find meaningful. The same goes for humanists who find that a simple negation of belief in a deity is not enough to live life ethically and find that the progressive values of humanism complement their skepticism.

After speaking before dozens of groups with nearly all attendees happy to use multiple freethought identifiers, it's obvious to me that any search for purity of name for members of the nontheist movement is a losing battle that inevitably constrains the movement and prevents people who don't believe in a god, yet ascribe to religious traditions, from joining. At the end of the day, no matter what self-identifying term(s) they employ, as long as people aren't expecting divine intervention, they are already acting as atheists. And those who want to emphasize the positive ideals they stand for readily embrace humanism.

If the nontheist movement is willing to accept people from all identities who are also not theistic, the movement will grow by leaps and bounds. Not only will this expanded pool build numbers, those who are still participating in faith institutions will help, from the inside, to make them more rational and humanistic than they are today. Their rejection of supernatural and dogmatic authoritarianism will also make the world a better place. We should respect humanist-leaning religious people who do not like the atheist label. Even though they may choose to identify and participate in a particular faith tradition, either because of their culture, their family, or some other societal reason, they also could be invited to identify as nontheistic humanists. Let's not create a schism where it isn't needed, and instead, let's be welcoming to those who wish to learn more about humanism and how to live a good life without a belief in a god.

How Do You Want to Be Represented?

When we take the conclusions above to heart and apply them to how we'd like to be represented by organizations like the American Humanist Association, we can see why member-driven campaigns have been so successful.

When the holiday advertising campaigns the American Humanist Association ran in DC, New York, and elsewhere featured the text: "Just Be Good for Goodness' Sake" alongside "Why Believe in a God?" or alongside "No God? No Problem!" most people saw these campaigns for what they were: an attempt to raise the flag for nontheists who focus on doing good and attract likely humanists. The reactions from religious and nonreligious were mostly positive. But, as absurd as it sounds, a surprising number of conservative religious people are convinced that these forms of outreach are aimed at them and are an underhanded attempt to convert them to atheism.

While this phenomenon of fundamentalists misinterpreting our intent may have more to do with the failings of the religious conservatives than it does us, it does raise some interesting questions. Is it worth risking offense to spread the freethought message? Can we be clear about our identity without alienating our progressive religious allies? As we continue to expand our positive impact on the world and increase the respect and acceptance of our worldview, the answer to both of these questions must be—Yes!

In past decades, we've seen some in our movement willing to "pass" as something we're not in order not to offend and to gain a sense of acceptance—a false sense of acceptance. It's time we come out of the closet.

That doesn't mean that we aim to purposely offend mainstream religious people. That wouldn't be consistent with humanism. If we really want to raise our profile, we need to continue our outreach and activism. And we should be clear about who we are, not for the purpose of offending people, but regardless of whether our very existence does cause offense.

The Case for Empathy

In arguing for humanism, we're not just arguing for discarding faith. Humanism is much more. Much of humanism's compassion, egalitarianism, and positive agenda foundationally derive from empathy.

Empathy is both an ability and a feeling. It's the ability to understand and share in the feelings of others almost as if you are experiencing their situation yourself. It's also the very feeling that one gets and the knowledge one acquires through this process. Since this may be the most powerfully positive force in existence, it deserves a deeper discussion than was provided in the introductory remarks about its role as a founding principle of humanism.

The empathy we experience when we place ourselves in another's shoes and imagine our own perspective in that situation is exceeded by the empathy we feel by truly understanding how the other person is feeling in their experience of the situation. Through empathy we're also able to perceive just how our behavior impacts other people.

This is seen most easily in its negative form when people fail to employ empathy. All too frequently this is prevalent in the closest of relationships such as that between parent and child. In the film *Dead Poets Society*, the character of Neil Perry (played by Robert Sean Leonard) struggles with his father (Kurtwood Smith) who is domineering in his pursuit of his own goals for Neil—so much so that he erupts in anger at Neil's interest in poetry and acting and plans to withdraw Neil from his liberal arts education and force him to attend a military academy. Unable to cope with his father's increasing demands for conformance, Neil ultimately takes his own life with his father's gun. Neil's father consistently fails to employ empathy and fails to understand that his own hopes and dreams for his son are not a shared vision. Even after the suicide, Mr. Perry persists in his disconnect and blames Mr. Keating (Robin Williams), Neil's creative and inspiring English teacher.

Humanist and clinical psychologist Leon Seltzer describes how empathy helps heal couples' relationships: "Through developing a greater understanding—and acceptance—of the other's nature and concerns (brought about through each spouse's increased empathy toward the other), their problems aren't so much resolved as they are transcended." Seltzer captures the situation very well in highlighting that empathy itself may not make problems go away. But the recognition of each other's perspective through empathy, and how that perspective connects to their good will and humanity, helps us rise above our difficulties.

By walking in another's shoes we gain insights into perspectives other than our own. When trying to muddle through a complex concept, empathy helps us step outside our preconceptions and personal limitations and see an idea from another's viewpoint. Moreover, empathy and altruism helped us advance as a species—it was survival for those who would look out for each other. We'd do well to remember this on a global scale as we confront challenges to our very existence.

Think about this in the context of understanding political theories. By learning about atheist author Richard Wright's time and experience, we can see how he came to initially embrace communism and continued to see socialist approaches as the only way to begin to level a radically uneven playing field. Similarly, by learning about atheist author Ayn Rand's time and experience, we might see how she saw the world through a completely different viewpoint, one that emphasizes objectivism and rational economic self-interest as the highest aim. Utilizing empathy to help us understand these political theories doesn't mean that we agree with them. In fact, actual attempts to implement communist and objectivist ideas betray just how far removed they are from humanism. But it gives us a more complete starting point to develop our own conclusions about how societies should best function.

Interestingly, evidence indicates that empathy is developed in the human animal more so than in others—even our closest cousins. A 2012 study, reported in *Nature,* reveals that children and chimpanzees both grasp the idea that they could work together to achieve a reward, but only the children grasped the concept that the sharing of such a collaboratively achieved award should be equal. Unlike the chimps, even if one child picked up more of the reward, they'd share it with the others. This indicates the further developed moral sense within humans. It demonstrates the empathetic understanding along with the compassionate action that flows from it when we have the strength to act. In this case, it indicates the understanding that all deserve appropriate rewards for their labors, and if one unfairly gets more, it's worth resetting the scales.

In 1933, Albert Einstein wrote: "There is one thing we do know: that we are here for the sake of others—above all for those upon whose smile and well-being our own happiness depends, and also for the countless unknown souls with whose fate we are connected by a bond of sympathy. Many times a day I realize how much my own life is built upon the labors of my fellows, and how earnestly I must exert myself in order to give in return as much as I have received."

Through empathy, we learn what it feels like to experience realities we haven't even faced, giving us a chance to learn from trial and error without the trial. That's a tremendous advantage, and the more we cultivate it, the more we benefit personally and as a society. In *The Better Angels of Our Nature,* 2006 Humanist of the Year Steven Pinker explains how we're progressing to a better and less violent world community. He highlights cosmopolitanism as a key force in this shift, a cosmopolitanism that he defines as something that "can prompt people to take the perspectives of people unlike themselves and to expand their circle of sympathy to embrace them"—essentially an expression of empathy. Without this crucial ability, people are limited to what they can perceive about the world on their own. They are at the mercy of their many ignorances and fears, and ultimately, it's not just they who suffer but society as a whole. It makes sense for leaders of thought and politics to do everything possible to cultivate a world where empathy is strengthened.

Positive Applications

In examining the argument for humanism, it's worth considering the commitment to reason and empathy. But it's also worth looking at the applications of such a worldview and what practical results one might expect. While applications will be discussed in detail in the next part, it's worth a preview here.

For starters, accepting a humanist worldview naturally leads many people to a variety of progressive conclusions. Humanism doesn't dogmatically require a stringent set of beliefs, but there is value in seeing the writing on the wall. Just being nonreligious makes one statistically more liberal than one's religious counterparts, but the numbers show self-identified humanists as considerably to the left of just about every group. This shouldn't be a surprise.

From what we've learned about humanist commitment to reason and empathy, and the compassion and egalitarianism that flow from those commitments, it's not hard to guess that humanists wouldn't accept outdated religious reasoning for discriminatory policies. Humanists embrace the scientific evidence around human-caused climate change and accept responsibility for our planet's future. And humanists utterly reject the merging of church and state in the public sphere.

Religion supports emotional needs in a way that may be reassuring: "God has a plan, God is watching over you, and Heaven is waiting for you." But ultimately it's a false reassurance based on nothing more than wishful thinking. Humanism offers reassurance by explaining that we have birthrights that don't have to be earned but are part of what it means to be human. Knowledge of the world shows us that even in bad situations we have the ability to bounce back, to improve ourselves and work through our predicaments. And even if there isn't anyone on high, watching over us, we have each other.

Humanists see the positive potential of this philosophy and are seeking to benefit society through its application in politics and daily life. Without running afoul our own commitment to keeping matters of religion and government separate, the American

Humanist Association developed a useful set of principles for character development that can be used in public and private schools—the *Ten Commitments: Guiding Principles for Teaching Values*, which is included in the appendices. Unlike the Ten Commandments, they don't prescribe religious doctrine, invite divisiveness, or treat women as property, and do much more than address murder, theft, dishonesty, and sexual fidelity.

Building on the ideas in the preceding section on empathy, we recognized that schools are responsible for developing literate and skilled human beings, but if we want society to progress, they also need to help their students develop good personal, social, and citizenship values. That's why the *Ten Commitments: Guiding Principles for Teaching Values* emphasizes altruism, caring for the world around us, critical thinking, empathy, ethical development, global awareness, humility, peace and social justice, responsibility, service, and participation. These commitments are not just for school children but are valuable for families and people of all ages.

Past AHA executive director Tony Hileman explained how being a humanist means living on the creative edge of our culture:

> Our culture is created and re-created in a continuing process of sometimes barely discernible steps that repeatedly replace the misconceptions and mythologies of one age with the understandings and rationality of another. This in turn changes our view of the world which again causes change which in turn results in the creation of yet another new culture. This rotation, this cycle can be a delightful and dizzying upward spiral, but it doesn't happen by itself—we have to work at it.
>
> There comes a point in this cycle of change, as we push back the frontier of the known, when we realize that what we've held as rational has become rationalization. There comes a point where we once again uncover in our think-

ing a mythology masquerading as rationality. That point, that instant of realization, exists on the creative edge of our culture.

As Hileman notes, humanists are ahead of the cultural curve. It's why we were among the first to support many now popular causes as we'll see in the coming chapters. It means that we may not always be regarded as having the same perspective as that of the majority. Being a humanist means accepting that responsibility for leadership, and knowing that one is often going to find oneself with a minority viewpoint, but also knowing that our commitment to advocacy means we're likely to steadily move society in the directions we seek to take it. A review of the history of modern humanism demonstrates the accuracy of this observation.

CHAPTER 4

Planting the Seeds

Humanism has an impressive history. With deep roots in the early Greek philosophers and in Eastern thinkers well before them, humanism grew during the Renaissance. It continued to develop throughout the Reformation, Enlightenment, and scientific revolution and began to take its present shape in the late nineteenth century. As it took its present form it drew in knowledge and wisdom from still more sources—from the historied lessons of Hán Yù, to the reason of Thomas Paine, to the leadership of Jawaharlal Nehru, to the steadfast action of Steve Biko, to the enduring example of Gloria Steinem.

Today humanism is expressed in many forms around the globe, sometimes building on past efforts, and sometimes springing forth independently. Non-religious Nelson Mandela expressed his humanism as *ubuntu*. A Nguni Bantu word translated as "humanity toward others," ubuntu incorporates aspects of sharing, community, respect, caring, trust, and unselfishness. Humanism crosses cultural and geographical boundaries because its essence in empathetic, egalitarian application of reason is truly universal.

The history of humanism is the story of a gradual formation and promotion of ideals and values that have persisted through the ages and became a major cultural and intellectual force in modern times. In the United States, the culmination of these principles expressed itself in the development and progress of the American Humanist Association, which has become a wellspring of ideas so powerful and relevant to the times that it has formed the seeds of new organizations that continue to exist and prosper.

The primary origins of what we now call humanism date back with particular relevancy to Renaissance Italy. It was this time of immense cultural, artistic, and educational discovery and advancement when both new and long-forgotten modes of thought began to flourish. This marked the end of the old medieval systems and the beginning of our modern world. It was here that humanist thought—focused on reason and experience—became widespread, helping to establish a philosophical presence making future organization of these emerging ideas possible.

The first Renaissance humanist was Francesco Petrarca, or Petrarch, who was poet laureate of Rome in 1341 and is considered the "father" of the Renaissance. Spanning several centuries, the Renaissance reached its pinnacle in central Europe before the turn of the eighteenth century as poets, artists, and intellectuals pursued a renewed passion for the arts and the philosophical concepts of the Greek and Roman classical periods. Theological thinkers like Erasmus brought a more human focus to religion. Sculptors and painters like Michelangelo brought it to the arts, and Shakespeare made it come alive in literature. In the seventeenth and eighteenth centuries critical minds like John Locke, Jean-Jacques Rousseau, and Voltaire advanced the idea that human reason alone could fight the social problems of ignorance, superstition, and tyranny. Such thinking was the herald of the Enlightenment, which challenged outmoded religion and the dominance of hereditary aristocracy. Moving forward, these humanistic underpinnings continued to impact the intellectual and political leaders of the original British colonies, leading to the founding of the United States.

During the nineteenth century these ideas were put to work in social movements that brought about the abolition of slavery, emancipation of women, mitigation of poverty, development of public health, and expansion of education. As an outgrowth of this temper, a formal, unified movement placing "deed before creed" originated in the United States during the end of the nineteenth and early part of the twentieth century. In 1876, Felix Adler founded the New York Society for Ethical Culture, which prompted the creation of similar ethical societies in Chicago, Philadelphia, and St. Louis. This new Ethical Culture movement not only fostered the founding of such reform efforts as the Legal Aid Society and the National Association for the Advancement of Colored People (NAACP), it helped establish humanism as a modern term.

Meanwhile, beginning in 1927, a number of Unitarian professors and students at the University of Chicago who had moved away from theism organized the Humanist Fellowship. Soon they launched the *New Humanist* magazine, offering a path forward for the Unitarian movement. But most of the other church members were still thinking in terms of a capital "G" God as the glue necessary to bind ideas to people and people to each other.

Around the same time, Charles Francis Potter founded the First Humanist Society of New York. Formerly a Baptist and then a Unitarian minister, Potter began the society with the intent of it being a religious organization, calling humanism "a new faith for a new age." Prominent members of this community included John Dewey, Julian Huxley, and Albert Einstein. Potter wrote a book entitled *Humanism: A New Religion*, outlining the basic premise and points of what he termed religious humanism. His philosophy openly rejected traditional Christian beliefs and replaced them with a humanist philosophy that incorporated various aspects of naturalism, materialism, rationalism, and socialism. And unlike common religious ideas of the time, Potter's intent was to offer an ever-evolving philosophy that would update itself as new knowledge was gained.

A major humanist milestone was achieved in 1933 when *A Humanist Manifesto* was written through the collaboration and agreement of thirty-four national leaders, including philosopher psychologist John Dewey and Unitarian author Lester Mondale. This was a publicly signed document detailing the basic tenets of humanism. By 1935 the Humanist Fellowship was supplanted by the Humanist Press Association, publisher of the *New Humanist* and the *Humanist Bulletin*.

The American Humanist Association (AHA) was formed in 1941, when Curtis W. Reese and John H. Dietrich, two well-known Unitarian ministers and humanists, reorganized the Humanist Press Association in Chicago, into the American Humanist Association.

The goal was not to establish a religion as Potter had originally intended but instead to recognize the nontheistic and secular nature of humanism, organize its advocates, and align the organization for the mutual education of both its religious and nonreligious members. This makes the American Humanist Association the oldest organization addressing the breadth of humanism in the United States. The AHA began publishing the *Humanist* magazine as the successor to the earlier publications, setting out to explore modern philosophical, cultural, social, and political issues from a humanist point of view.

Active from an early stage, Unitarian minister Edwin H. Wilson was selected as the first executive director of the AHA with the primary job of producing the magazine. At this time he was also minister of an Ohio Unitarian church, and he established a printing company for the magazine in Yellow Springs, Ohio, a small town with a long Quaker history and the home of Antioch College.

Within the first decade, philosopher Corliss Lamont (later author of *The Philosophy of Humanism*) became involved and contributed funds to advance the organization in a more significant way. Lamont spent much of the 1940s and 50's challenging Senator Joseph McCarthy and the House Un-American Activities Committee. He held to the position that despite the prevailing "Red Scare" anti-communist attitude, the United States should try to maintain a productive relationship with the Soviet Union. As a result of this position, and his generally liberal thinking, he became a target of government, had his passport illegally confiscated, and had his mail intercepted. But, as he details in his book *Freedom Is As Freedom Does*, Lamont fought back in the courts and won.

And with Lamont's financial help, a small office of unique design was built a few blocks from Antioch College where Wilson began working full-time, and the AHA gradually grew in significance.

At the end of the 1940s, the organization was supportive of Vashti McCollum in her fight against religious instruction in public schools. The mother of two boys, McCollum argued that religious instruction in public education violated the principle of separation of church and state. Her case traveled all the way to the US Supreme Court where, in 1948, she achieved a watershed ruling in her favor. In 1962, McCollum became the first woman to serve as AHA president—long before a number of Christian denominations began to ordain women.

In 1952 the AHA became a founding member of the International Humanist and Ethical Union (IHEU) in Amsterdam, Netherlands. With national membership groups in dozens of countries, the IHEU continues to be the organization providing an international forum for humanist groups worldwide. It also represents a global humanist movement with adherents numbering in the millions, bringing humanist values to bear at the United Nations and other international organizations.

During the 1950s, readers of the *Humanist* would sometimes contact the AHA saying they wanted to get together with others who shared their values. They were initially directed to their local Unitarian church to help build or expand a core of humanists there. However, some had no interest in going to a place where an intervening god, and even the Christian Bible was often the core of the Sunday sermon. Though the forgoing was often done in an enlightened, progressive, non-supernatural context, it still was not what most humanists were seeking. Eventually a procedure was established to certify local AHA chapters, but there wasn't funding at first to provide them guidance or support.

The AHA was governed at this time by a member-elected board of directors that increasingly grew more interested in promoting humanism and less interested in tying it to the Unitarian movement. When Wilson moved on from the AHA, he founded a group now known as the Unitarian Universalist Humanist Association. The AHA board hired Tolbert McCarroll as the new executive director. McCarroll worked to re-focus the AHA to better support chapters and affiliates (there are over 200 as of 2016) and make the AHA relevant as its own organization. He also initiated the Humanist Celebrant program, which enables humanists to be endorsed to officiate weddings and other services.

Running parallel with this localizing and personalizing of the humanist philosophy was the empowerment of women within the organization. The second editor of the *Humanist* was Priscilla Robertson, whose work began in 1956. One of the earliest of the AHA's Humanists of the Year was Margaret Sanger who received that award in 1957, honored for her activism for birth control and sex education. But Sanger was just the first of many of the leading feminist and reproductive rights activists to work closely with the AHA. Just among those in this category who received the AHA's top award were Mary Calderone and Betty Friedan in the 1970s, Faye Wattleton and Margaret Atwood in the 1980s, Alice Walker and Barbara Ehrenreich in the 1990s, and most recently Gloria Steinem in 2012.

In the 1960s, the AHA was active in challenging the illegality of abortion. It was the first national membership organization to support abortion rights, even before Planned Parenthood expanded to address the issue. Humanists were instrumental in the founding of leading pro-choice organizations such as the Religious Coalition for Reproductive Choice and NARAL Pro-Choice America. These organizations continue to defend and support elective abortion rights.

During this time, the AHA and the American Ethical Union (AEU, the national organization for Ethical Culture) joined efforts on behalf of nontheistic conscientious objectors to the Vietnam War. The two groups also worked together to create the first nationwide memorial societies in order to give people access to inexpensive alternatives to mortuary burial. Today cremation and humanistic memorial services are more widely available and affordable than ever before.

A number of other developments highlight this intriguing time. A local humanist leader in California, Maulana Karenga, was jailed for his civil rights activism, and during that sentence he created an AHA prison chapter and significantly advanced his idea for the current national holiday of Kwanzaa. The first effort to coordinate and initiate student and youth activities was launched as an AHA project called the Humanist Student Union of North America (HSUNA). In 1969 (through 1977) the AHA and the AEU jointly published the *Humanist* magazine. And during the 1970s the AHA shared the Joint Washington Office for Social Concern with the American Ethical Union and the Unitarian Universalist Association.

Polio vaccine developer Jonas Salk was the 1976 Humanist of the Year at a time when humanism was achieving a high point of respectability in intellectual circles.

James Farmer
Ernest Nagel
Jonas Salk
Henry Morgantaler

1976, 35th Annual Conference
Buffalo, New York

Humanism and the AHA reached another milestone during the 1970s when the AHA released a major new humanist text, *Humanist Manifesto II*. Drafted by Edwin H. Wilson and Paul Kurtz, the work was released during Labor Day weekend in 1973 to unprecedented media fanfare. The *New York Times* interviewed Kurtz after the AHA submitted a pre-publication press release announcing the new work. Following the interview, the *Times* published an in-depth, front-page article exploring humanist philosophy and the new manifesto. This article created a deluge of coverage in major publications around the world. Welcomed by many commentators, the manifesto was denounced by the religious conservatives as anti-religious and anti-God. Regardless, *Humanist Manifesto II* was a monumental achievement for the AHA in its goal to spread humanism to the public.

Following this release, the AHA continued on its energized path of starting new endeavors and publishing major statements. The AHA created the Committee for the Scientific Investigation of Claims of the Paranormal, which founded a journal called *Skeptical Inquirer*. Eventually the committee branched off as a separate organization that continues to this day to challenge various forms of pseudoscience around the world.

The AHA's major statements at the time, included:

- *A Plea for Beneficent Euthanasia* challenged current prohibitions on voluntary euthanasia and called for "a more enlightened public opinion to transcend traditional taboos and move in the direction of a compassionate view toward needless suffering in dying." The document was signed by medical, legal, and religious leaders and brought the idea of death with dignity into the public sphere where it continues to be discussed and debated today.

- *Objections to Astrology* was signed by 186 leading scientists, including eighteen Nobel Prize winners; its intent was to aid consumers in rejecting this pseudoscience.

- *A New Bill of Sexual Rights and Responsibilities* set out to illustrate and celebrate responsible sexual freedom without the shackles and control from church or state. The issues were widely debated and the publication received coverage in *Time* magazine.

- *A Statement Affirming Evolution as a Principle of Science* was published in 1977 and mailed to every major school district in the country, solidifying the AHA as a key proponent of evolution over creationism.

- *A Declaration for Older Persons* called for an end to age discrimination in the workplace. It was signed by members of Congress, labor leaders, business executives, and religious leaders. Resulting from the AHA's efforts, much of what this document suggested has become national law.

As the AHA approached its fortieth year of operation, it began publishing the *Creation/Evolution* journal, a unique periodical founded by Fred Edwords and focused on countering the arguments of the so-called "scientific" creationists. The journal was published through the decade and was then purchased by the new National Center for Science Education in 1991. That organization continued to publish it internationally before ultimately blending it into *Reports of the National Center for Science Education*, continuing to offer facts and arguments in opposition to creationism and in support of quality science education.

The 1980s saw the beginning of an onslaught of attacks by the Religious Right against secular humanism and the AHA. In an attempt to counter the smears, the AHA began its own campaign, which included media appearances, public debates, nationally-published articles, press conferences, lobbying, and legal action. Interested in this debate, world-renowned author Isaac Asimov joined in as the elected president of the AHA in 1985.

Through the work of Jack and Lois Trimpey, the AHA advanced Rational Recovery, an organization devoted to helping people with addictions. From Rational Recovery and the work of Joseph Gerstein emerged the very effective SMART Recovery, based on the Rational-Emotive Behavior Therapy of noted humanist psychologist Albert Ellis. REBT, as it's termed, is an action-oriented approach that teaches individuals how to replace irrational, self-defeating thoughts, feelings, and actions with rational, self-affirming thoughts, feelings, and actions. This empowering psychological system is devoid of religious or supernatural influence.

Along with Albert Ellis, psychologists and psychiatrists including Erich Fromm, Abraham Maslow, B.F. Skinner, Carl Rogers, and Rudolf Dreikurs all wrote extensively on humanism throughout the twentieth century.

As the AHA celebrated its fiftieth anniversary in 1991, the *Humanist* became a major alternative medium for social and political commentary. Through such efforts, the magazine has attracted and published the writing of such luminaries as Alice Walker, Lester R. Brown, Aung Sung Suu Kyi, Noam Chomsky, Kate Michelman, Dan Rather, Ted Turner, and many other leading journalists, writers, political leaders, and activists.

Kurt Vonnegut was named Humanist of the Year in 1992 and went on to become the AHA's honorary president. Always true to his character, Vonnegut wrote a decade later to the AHA offices: "Find here my permission for you to quote any damn fool thing I've ever said or written, through all eternity, and without further notice or compensation to me."

228 E. 48 NYC 10017
Nov. 15, 2003

DEAR FRED EDWORDS —
FIND HERE MY PERMISSION FOR YOU TO QUOTE ANY DAMN FOOL THING I'VE EVER SAID OR WRITTEN, THROUGH-OUT ALL ETERNITY, AND WITHOUT ANY FURTHER NOTICE OR COMPENSATION TO ME.

81 AS OF 11/11/03

In 1995, the AHA took part in issuing *Religion in the Public Schools: A Joint Statement of Current Law,* which gave teachers and administrators a practical guide to what they could and could not do with religion in the public schools. The AHA joined a variety of other organizations and religious groups to release this primer, which influenced the policies of President Bill Clinton, was used by schools across the country, and was frequently cited in news reports on the issue years after publication.

The AHA was one of the first organizations to become fully active online with the introduction of its website in 1995. It remains a leader in online and social media communications with hundreds of thousands of followers throughout its active presence on Facebook, Twitter, Instagram, Google+, and its online magazine theHumanist.com.

Beginning in 1998, humanist leadership became involved in a new way to bring young people into the humanist movement through Camp Quest. As longtime challengers of the Boy Scouts of America's exclusionary policies toward nontheists (both in and out of the courts), the AHA was pleased to provide multiple scholarships for a nondiscriminatory camp retreat for children. Camp Quest became fully independent as its own corporation in 2002 and now has over a dozen locations in the United States and other countries, serving over a thousand kids each summer.

One of the AHA leadership's biggest decisions was to move the organization to Washington DC. Previously the AHA had moved from Yellow Springs, Ohio, to San Francisco, California, to Amherst, New York. Matters of convenience and economy had dictated the selection of each of these locations. But now the organization made a strategic choice:

A move to Washington DC would take humanism to the center of power and influence.

This wouldn't have been possible without the full agreement of the trustees of the AHA's endowment fund, now called the Humanist Foundation, since they provided the funding, along with a seed grant from Lloyd Morain, for a building in the heart of the nation's capital. Relocation to the new Humanist Center was completed in 2002 under the leadership of Executive Director Tony Hileman. Through this move, the AHA was empowered to substantially increase the humanist voice in the public debate.

The philosophy of humanism itself took a major evolutionary step in 2003 with the release of *Humanism and its Aspirations*, the third humanist manifesto, signed by two dozen Nobel Prize winners. More concise than its two predecessors, the third manifesto set out to continue the trend of clarifying the humanist philosophy in a way that paid tribute to core humanist values while challenging humanists to take action toward making this world a better place.

It was in DC where the AHA began to take advantage of best non-profit practices, achieving full ratings by charitable accountability organizations such as the Better Business Bureau, Charity Navigator, and GuideStar. The AHA maintained and improved the *Humanist* magazine, created the *Free Mind* newsletter for its members, and added the *Essays in the Philosophy of Humanism* peer-reviewed journal.

The AHA then got ahead of the curve online again by first taking over the Institute for Humanist Studies' (a humanist organization founded by philanthropist Larry Jones and based in Albany, New York) podcast and e-zine and then launching *TheHumanist.com* as the first daily original content online news site for the movement. The Humanist Press publishing arm, founded in 1995, was re-launched in 2012 with a focus on bringing humanist voices to a larger market online by adding multiple well-reviewed titles every year.

In 2005, AHA board members had the creative concept of attempting the first movement-coordinated advertising campaign. Highlighting the benefits of mass media advertising as a way to reach people, no one initially realized how big an idea this would become. The first campaign ran in a series of progressive magazines, such as *The Nation* and the *American Prospect*, and had a mild message where everyday people cited their good values and concluded with, "I'm a humanist!" What was unexpected was that the campaign attracted some modest press attention that doubled the number of people who saw the ads.

From there it wasn't long before we fully took advantage of how many people we could reach through advertising. In November 2008 came the AHA's holiday ad campaign, the first of this kind of approach in the United States, where we labeled the sides of buses with slogans like, "Why Believe in a God? Just Be Good for Goodness' Sake." This brought in media attention worth millions of dollars and its success ignited annual holiday campaigns by multiple movement organizations from that day forward.

That same year, AHA's billboard message "Don't Believe in God? You are Not Alone" generated ten times the visibility that a typical billboard would attract. Soon it was expanded through a new program, launched in March 2009, called the United Coalition of Reason, founded by Steve Rade, AHA's 2014 Humanist Business Leader. This funded ads in scores of media markets to help bring together the local secular, atheist, humanist, ethical, and freethought groups that already existed. It was a boon for all levels of the movement, stimulating attention, organization, and coordination as never before.

While more strident ads received attention, it was the simplest that seemed best. Just "One Nation Indivisible" on a flag background (instead of the Pledge of Allegiance's "one nation, under God, indivisible") yielded international press coverage for the North Carolina Secular Association in 2010. And the ads continued with the first coordinated radio effort and then the AHA's "Consider Humanism" campaign in 2008, which compared Bible quotes with humanist quotes to emphasize a more inclusive, progressive morality. This included the first-ever nationwide network TV commercial from the nontheist movement.

Ads weren't the only big changes in the AHA. The gradual conversion of the organization, from a merely philosophically forward-looking organization to its current capability to actually accomplish humanistic change, created a new environment. Two leading investors in humanism, each coming from different but compatible perspectives, jumpstarted these new capabilities. Lou Appignani took the perspective of a humanism stepping forward with a clear atheist perspective, whereas Pritpal Kochhar envisioned humanists leading the way even within religious communities. With both on board, the AHA was able to keep its tent big enough for the full breadth of humanism.

To ensure that the constitutional rights of humanists would be represented in court, the AHA launched the Appignani Humanist Legal Center in 2007. Through amicus brief activity, litigation, and other legal advocacy, this legal arm is now actively involved in church-state separation cases, nontheistic equal protection lawsuits, and the full range of humanist issues. Utilizing a strategy of combining staff lawyers with scores of mobilized pro-bono attorneys nationwide, the Humanist Legal Center has racked up an impressive win/loss ratio where almost every involvement leads to success. In 2013 when the case against "under God" in the Pledge of Allegiance reached the Massachusetts Supreme Judicial Court, the AHA's caseload dramatically expanded as a result of the attention, and the Humanist Legal Center expanded to continue supporting the growing base of clients.

Efforts to remove "under God" stepped up another level when the AHA launched the Boycott the Pledge campaign to encourage folks to actively challenge the religious language in the Pledge by legally sitting it out in protest. With kids and adults across the nation opting out of the Pledge, the caseload and win rate of the legal center continued to rise. Teachers illegally admonished students for not participating in the Pledge. In one case in North Dakota, a six-year old boy was lifted out of his seat by the teacher to force his participation. In another case in Pennsylvania a middle school girl who opted out was refused medical treatment from the school nurse. While the experience for most participants in the boycott was empowering whether or not they had a situation to contend with, it's shocking how many schools are unaware of the legal right to not participate in the Pledge that the Supreme Court made clear in the 1943 case *West Virginia State Board of Ed. v. Barnette*.

In 2008 humanist education got a boost with the AHA's establishment of the Kochhar Humanist Education Center. After study and pilot efforts, it published guides for establishing humanist education programs for both children and adults. These guides, supplemented with more material online and offline, helped local groups set up their programming. The KHEC also brought together a Humanist Teacher Corps to develop curriculum, present on positive principles, and be advocates for well-rounded curricula and textbooks in the public schools. And the Paths to Humanism project was initiated to develop introductions to humanism from the perspective of the world's various religious traditions. By this means, the AHA provides a bridge for those who are essentially humanists but identify with a traditional faith—if that sounds confusing, think of them as atheists who happen to go to church, and by the numbers, there's a great deal of them.

Through the addition of The Humanist Institute as an affiliate, the AHA now has a graduate level program in humanism, increasing the preparation of future humanist leaders. The Humanist Institute also offers a plethora of online courses in humanism and trainings for Humanist Celebrants and activists called the Kochhar Online Humanist Education program. It also prepares in-person trainings for key humanist functions such as officiating weddings or conducting funerals. Those interested in expanding their involvement in the humanist movement might wish to participate in what The Humanist Institute has to offer.

The Center for Freethought Equality is the AHA's lobbying arm and employs a full-time lobbyist who is active daily on Capitol Hill. In 2011, the Center helped write the first part of a bill from the humanist movement ever sponsored in the House—the Darwin Day resolution. With the help of the Secular Coalition for America, it was sponsored in the Senate as well in 2015. The Darwin Day resolution, which has attracted increasing numbers of co-sponsors, seeks to make Charles Darwin's birthday a nationally-recognized observance and to emphasize the teaching of science over creationism and the so-called intelligent design movement. Parallel to this effort, AHA also administers the Darwin Day Foundation, which now provides resources for hundreds of local Darwin Day events.

The Center for Freethought Equality also has a political action committee called the Freethought Equality Fund (FEF PAC). Since it doesn't take long in Washington to learn that those who have political action committees capable of making contributions to help elect sympathetic candidates get taken a lot more seriously than those who don't, it was time to get involved in elections. The FEF PAC exists "to change the face of American politics and to achieve equality by increasing the number of open humanists and atheists in public office at all levels of government." The FEF PAC provides nontheistic Americans the opportunity to make their voices heard in the political process by supporting candidates who identify as humanist, atheist, or agnostic—as well as supporting those who share the goals of protecting the separation of church and state and defending the civil liberties of secular Americans.

The AHA also launched and expanded other programs during this time. The LGBTQ Humanist Alliance boosted local LGBTQ activism among humanists and attracted AHA awardees Candace Gingrich-Jones, George Takei, Greta Christina, and Dan Savage to the organization. The the AHA similarly reorganized the Feminist Humanist Alliance and launched the Black Humanist Alliance in 2016 to deepen the involvement on social justice issues. And the AHA participates in nontheistic coalitions like the Secular Coalition for America and the International Humanist and Ethical Union as well as several issue-based coalitions addressing everything from torture to reproductive rights.

AHA membership varied over the first six decades from two thousand to five thousand, and even Corliss Lamont thought it might never break six thousand, because he thought humanism's constantly forward-looking viewpoints would keep it beyond the reach of large numbers. But in its seventh decade, executive director Tony Hileman propelled AHA membership above the six thousand-member mark, breaking that apparent ceiling. In the following decade support took off—in 2014, the AHA counted thirty thousand members and supporters. Today, the AHA continues to attract like-minded people at a rapid rate and is still developing its growing variety of programs that make up its powerful activist agenda.

Looking ahead, the American Humanist Association, its members, chapters, affiliates, and publications vow to not only support and defend core humanist values but also to press the public to consider and discuss humanist issues and social concerns. Guided by reason and humanity's rapidly growing knowledge of the world, by ethics and compassion, and in the pursuit of fuller, more meaningful lives that add to the greater good of society and humanity, the members of the AHA envision a world of mutual care and concern where the lifestance of humanism is known and respected, and where people take responsibility for the world in which they live.

CHAPTER 5

Prejudice Humanists Face

The Christian Right in the United States

While it may come as no surprise that humanists face prejudice from fundamentalists, it's worth noting how deep-seated and pervasive it is. Though such opposition extends to a wide variety of faiths and dogmas, we see it primarily emanating from the Christian Right in the United States, a kind of fundamentalism inherently opposed to humanism on many levels.

Foundationally, fundamentalists believe that all goodness derives from their god, so the presence of anyone being good without their god is a constant reminder that something is wrong with their belief on the source of goodness. They fumble for other possibilities like the improbable idea that all atheists are bad or the absurd conclusion that atheists don't exist and instead, that atheists have just deluded themselves into thinking they are atheists. That's why fundamentalists react with such remarkable aversion and hate when confronted with the AHA's simple GOOD WITHOUT A GOD stickers, advertisements, and billboards. It's why they so vehemently characterize our positive personal statement as a personal attack on them.

Any positive gesture or even self-defense for nontheists is an automatic attack on the core belief of this type of theist who insists that goodness comes only from their god.

In interviews with conservative hosts from minor local talk shows all the way to CNN, I've experienced that hatred, sometimes directly and sometimes as part of the character these media personalities developed. The smaller venues are where I most often have seen people express their real fear of atheists and what productive atheism means for their often unproductive prayerful efforts. I recall one local radio host, broadcasting to the town I lived in at the time, exclaimed that people like me shouldn't exist. I became a little alarmed as he called for something to be done about people like me. But when he closed with saying, "You'll get yours in the afterlife," I was relieved. As long as he doesn't incite his right-wing followers to act in the here and now, I'm happy to take my chances and face whatever follows a long and happy humanist life.

Fox News commentators like Bill O'Reilly and Megyn Kelly have cultivated a persona that requires them to lash out at others to maintain their base. When the AHA ran the "Why believe in a god? Just be good for goodness' sake" bus advertisements in 2008, I was called to appear on CNN *Headline News* opposite the demagogue Catholic League President Bill Donohue. Donohue had the audacity to call our open-ended question "hate speech" while simultaneously comparing humanists to Jeffrey Dahmer and Adolf Hitler. He said that it was impossible to be good for goodness' sake and that our ad was a personal attack on his faith. Later, Bill O'Reilly insanely asked, "Why do they loathe the baby Jesus? You don't sell atheism by running down a baby!" How he leaps to these conclusions I'll never know, but I think it's more of an expression of their efforts to stir the bigotries of their followers rather than engage in meaningful debate.

But the fundamentalists' break with humanism extends far beyond the conundrum of our *godless goodness*. In desperately trying to hold on to their faith in the presence of the real world they occupy, they've had to draw lines in the sand before human evolution, elective abortion, same-sex marriage, and a whole slew of issues with which they are in direct opposition with humanists.

In order to avoid the daily confrontation with our position and risk the potential damage to their faith, their leadership goes to the extreme of trying to convert the United States into a Christian nation. As a tactic, they falsely proclaim that the United States was always a Christian nation even though it's easily disproven with facts about our nation's founders and the obvious lack of religious determinism in the US Constitution. The real story of our founding saw the Constitution shock the world by proclaiming that, in America, there would be no religious test for public office. Yet the Christian nation lie persists and is pushed at every opportunity, through their own advertising, which outnumbers ours at least a hundred to one, and through constant attempts to get the local, state, and national governments to recognize the Christian faith above other faiths and philosophies.

Until very recent years, there has been an inadequate response from our movement, allowing fundamentalists to piece together coalitions on many issues to give them a large enough voice to win the day in politics, the media, and often with the general public. Now we're fighting back against the Religious Right on many fronts.

Widespread Prejudice

In Sam Harris's *Letter to a Christian Nation*, he uncovered a dangerous weapon that the Religious Right had been wielding against both the religious and the secular left for years. By convincing mainstream people of faith, and even many secularists, that critique of religion was inherently wrong, the religious extremists in our midst got a free pass to hate whoever they wish, discriminate as they like, and seek laws that trample the rights of others—all free from criticism. For if it's taboo to criticize religion in politics, and just impolite to do it in circles where you'd have no problem engaging in friendly debates on other subjects, then such anti-humanist ideas and behavior go unchecked.

Fortunately, Harris exposed this situation in his bestselling book and our movement developed a stronger voice. But as we'll see, our move from a silent minority to a growing and increasingly more vocal one, also resulted in a backlash of more widespread prejudice.

Traditional religions and their beliefs in gods are on the decline in America no matter how you measure it. One in five Americans have no religion according to the Pew Forum on Religion and Public Life, fewer people attend religious services than they publicly claim according to the Public Religion Research Institute, and the number of open atheists has doubled since 2007 according to a Harris poll. All told, the roughly 15% of Americans who are nontheists represent more people than that of Muslims, Jews, Mormons, and Pentecostalists combined! That's more than the estimated gay and lesbian population, more even than the African American population. And all of these figures undoubtedly understate our true strength because of social pressure not to tell an interviewer that you're a nonbeliever. We are, in fact, one of the largest minorities in the US, but you'd never know it from our organized numbers or political power.

Political acceptance of atheism has lagged behind social acceptance with more than half of Americans saying that they wouldn't vote for an atheist candidate for president, according to a survey by Pew. And while we have one current member of Congress, Rep. Kyrsten Sinema, who chose to be sworn in on the Constitution instead of the Bible and who openly wrote that she is a "none" when it comes to religion, there are no members of Congress willing to publicly state that they don't happen to believe in a god since open humanist Rep. Pete Stark of California left office in 2013. When another humanist politician from Colorado, David Habecker, decided to exercise his right to not say the Pledge of Allegiance because of the words "under God" during a town trustees meeting, he suffered a recall election that threw him out of office. But he remained strong, telling those gathered at an AHA conference, "I am as much a patriot as any American; I honor and respect those whose shoulders we stand on. My bible is the Constitution; my faith is in its promise, truth, and the goodness of the human spirit."

Disturbingly, the Pew study cited above also shows that other "taboos" such as drug usage and adultery by a candidate are becoming more acceptable at a faster rate than atheism. What does it say about our country when we are willing to elect leaders who cheat and lie and break the law over atheists who live ethically? Do we as a nation truly believe that the theological beliefs of a candidate are more important than how that person actually lives their life? The answer for now is yes.

People who proclaim a belief in a deity are for some reason seen as more trustworthy and moral than those who don't, regardless of whether or not religious people actually live up to the values that they proclaim to be endorsed by their god. A study conducted at the University of British Columbia and the University of Oregon confirmed that this trust issue is at the root of anti-atheist prejudice—horrifyingly, even rapists share about the same level of trust. This is why people claim to attend religious services when they actually don't, because society reinforces the idea that being a religious person means that you are good and trustworthy. As Richard Dawkins quotes in *The God Delusion*, George H. W. Bush once said: "'No, I don't know that atheists should be considered as citizens, nor should they be considered patriots. This is one nation under God.'"

While this blind deferral towards religious people may change in the future because of shifting religious demographics, we must now grapple with the consequences of this prejudice. That means we will have to deal with legions of government officials who proclaim their faith as a virtue and publicly pray in order to prove their religious *bona fides*, even if they are nothing more than charlatans using religion as a cover for their personal failings. Unfortunately, too many voters aren't willing to look much deeper than the religious beliefs an individual professes when evaluating whether or not that person is ethical, so this religious masquerade is still an effective tool for those with a questionable history who want to be elected to public office.

It's useful to acknowledge that this pervasive hate actually takes a toll on us. Author Chris Stedman explores this subject in his interview of Melanie Brewster, editor of *Atheists in America* and Columbia University professor, for *Religion News Service*. In it we learn from Brewster that "people from marginalized groups—such as people of color, LGBTQs, and atheists—experience disproportionate stigma and, in turn, experience extra stress linked to their identities. This stress has been shown to cause depression, self-harm behaviors, substance abuse, body image issues, and more." Brewster is breaking new ground researching how atheists experience this minority stress.

Prejudice against atheists remains very real, and our political system is among the most open arenas in which it can be applied. At its root, the prejudice that persists against our community is the false idea that one cannot be good without a god, a myth perpetuated by those whose power derives from faith. We want to defeat those who would hold us back for personal gain and advance from today's intolerance toward tomorrow's tolerance of nontheists. We want to continue from that point to a time when there is mutual respect for our humanist viewpoints, and finally arrive at a day when there is a common appreciation for our reason and compassion-based, science-oriented approach to solving problems.

Today, Religious Right leaders have the power and influence to use the government to enforce laws that put truth claims about religion in front of us at every turn. Here are some distressing examples:

- Our children and grandchildren have to hear a statement that excludes them and their family every day at school, and if that weren't bad enough they're asked to stand and recite the statement along with the majority. Interestingly, current students' grandparents didn't have to endure this, as "under God" was only added to the Pledge of Allegiance in 1954.

- We must endure statements about our nation's trust in a fictional god, not just on our money, but also on public buildings, and in ceremonies for public office—from census worker to president.

- We have to watch as our neighbors go unpunished for child abuse because they claim a religious exemption to certain laws. Such exemptions also may apply to vaccinations that leave our children more vulnerable to disease.

- We have to spend our tax dollars on schools in most states where educators refuse to teach that the evidence massively supports a theory of evolution that unites everything we know about biology.

- When we're in the military we're in danger of harassment from not just our peers, but officers as well.

- We see federal funds used to repair churches that promote beliefs opposed to our own.

- Our kids are forced to use textbooks heavily influenced by the Religious Right.

- Our own representatives gratuitously blame us for tragedies like the Sandy Hook school shooting.

- Our tax dollars are spent on religious charitable organizations that refuse to employ us and even bar us from using their services.

- And, in certain communities, the more we come out of the closet as people who don't happen to believe in a god, the more we suffer new restrictions in our business opportunities and in public life.

But what's possibly worse is that the legal battles our broader movement is engaged in to improve our predicament are now losing at an unacceptable rate. This is even true when averaging in the AHA's Appignani Humanist Legal Center's excellent win rate.

Chipping Away at the Church-State Wall

Our movement used to be regularly successful arguing for the First Amendment principle of the separation of church and state, back in the days of Vashti McCollum's 1948 case that forbade using classrooms for religious instruction. We were successful back when Ellery Schempp's 1963 case forbade Bible readings in public schools as we were in a number of other important cases that challenged the teaching of creationism. But a great deal has changed since then.

For one, judges are less sympathetic to our cause than they used to be. This didn't happen by chance. When Michael Newdow's first case against "under God" in the Pledge of Allegiance was being considered in the Ninth Circuit Court of Appeals, President George W. Bush said, "It points up the fact that we need common-sense judges who understand that our rights were derived from God," implying that he intended to directly violate the Constitution where it says that there shall be no religious test for public office.

Then Bush ended a fifty-year history of using the advice of the American Bar Association (ABA) to consider judicial candidates, replacing the ABA's advice with that of the conservative Federalist Society. And unlike his predecessors, George W. went on to appoint primarily conservative Catholics and Christian evangelicals to the federal bench, stacking it against us and against any who want a strong First Amendment.

Unfortunately, the Religious Right understands all too well the power that money can have in politics. Groups like the Eagle Forum and Jay Sekulow's American Center on Law and Justice are extremely well-funded legal think tanks that have developed strategies to thwart our efforts. What's the result? Sadly, as a movement, we're losing more and more often.

The main problem with bringing Establishment Clause cases today is the legal doctrine of "standing." In order to ask the courts to hear your case, you have to prove standing by showing that (1) you've been wronged or injured, (2) that something can be done about it, and (3) that you are the right person or organization to bring the complaint. Normally, the injury you complain about has to be concrete and particular, so it wouldn't be enough to say generally: "I'm a taxpayer, and this government expenditure offends me." However, a "taxpayer standing" was made possible as a result of a case from the good old days when we most often won, and the Establishment Clause was better enforced.

In 1968, *Flast v. Cohen* recognized an exception to allow taxpayer standing for church-state cases, since otherwise there seemed to be almost no way to get the courts to hear them. The reason this is more of a problem today is that the *Flast* exception has been chipped away at in recent years. Now it's incredibly difficult to bring challenges under the Establishment Clause absent a "concrete" and "particularized injury." Here are a couple of relevant cases that got us to this point.

In the 1982 case of *Valley Forge Christian College v. Americans United for Separation of Church and State,* a portion of land from a closed army hospital was given to a Christian college, and Americans United (AU) sued. A split Supreme Court surprisingly ruled that AU didn't have standing to sue because the gift was made without regard to a decision by Congress. They said it was just an action by a government agency that didn't impact the taxing and spending power of government. As more conservative justices were added to the bench, our chances of success in this kind of case only went downhill.

That's why there was great concern in Washington, DC, when the Freedom From Religion Foundation (FFRF) challenged Jay F. Hein, director of the White House Office of Faith-Based Initiatives for holding conferences that favored religious organizations. Some believed that the only reason the Supreme Court would hear such a case was to further set back our cause. Indeed, in 2007, the Court denied taxpayer standing to FFRF and to any future federal taxpayers challenging the use of federal funds to support executive branch government actions. That means that the entire executive branch of government from the armed forces to the presidency itself are free from having to ever face nearly any lawsuit challenging their violations of the Establishment Clause. If brought with the argument of taxpayer standing, it would be automatically dismissed.

Supreme Court Justice David Souter argued in his dissent that "[w]hen executive agencies spend identifiable sums of tax money for religious purposes, no less than when Congress authorizes the same thing, taxpayers suffer injury," which makes sense. But who knows how long it will be before Justice Souter's opinion prevails?

Even in cases where plaintiffs do have standing, the courts are increasingly reluctant to rule on Establishment Clause grounds. The courts tend to justify government endorsement of religion as "accommodation," as historically acceptable ("ceremonial deism") or dismiss it as *de minimis* (such as "In God We Trust" challenges).

It's not just standing cases that we're losing. In *Salazar v. Buono* in 2010, the Supreme Court decided that it was constitutional to sell a tiny plot of public land where there might be a religious symbol in order to get around the fact that this was a public religious display.

In 2005, the Court ruled in *Cutter v. Wilkinson*, that the Religious Land Use and Institutionalized Persons Act (RLUIPA) allowed for more religious exceptions to secular rules. I call these "special rights for the religious" because they all allow religious people to opt out of the rules.

RLUIPA and the *Cutter v. Wilkinson* case made it worse. It used to be that the burden was on the individual to prove that the state was limiting their religious liberty. Now the individual is assumed correct, and it's the *government's* burden to prove that the exception requested caused a substantial problem for the state. By flipping the burden of proof to the government, it's much easier for the Religious Right to argue for all sorts of religious exceptions and special rights, which are multiplying faster than rabbits. They range from the right to wear a special hat in a driver's license photo or eat a special meal in prison, to truly substantive benefits such as getting tax-free housing allowances for their leaders, not vaccinating their kids, and getting free off-the-record counseling in the military.

Legal Discrimination

It was this same logic applied to the Religious Freedom Restoration Act that allowed the *Burwell v. Hobby Lobby* case in 2014 to open the doors to legal discrimination against nontheists and others.

Hobby Lobby was the first significant example of corporations trying to use their owners' religious beliefs in order to discriminate—free from criminal or civil penalties—against their own employees. Americans of all religions and of no religions should realize that religious liberty will only survive if we understand that the right to believe as one sees fit is paramount; it's not up to governments to become thought police. But when people act on what they perceive as the duties of their faith, such actions cannot interfere with the rights of others. When they do interfere, it ceases to be religious liberty and becomes religious imposition. In addition, government officials might use the logic from this case to refuse to work for the interests of religious and philosophical minorities because of their belief that those minorities are heretical and should be opposed.

If religious liberty becomes simply the right to act on one's prejudices free from consequences, as the *Hobby Lobby* decision implies, those of minority worldviews will find themselves in a situation similar to those faced prior to the founding of America. Humanists, Jews, Muslims, Buddhists and other religious and irreligious minorities will face increased discrimination, whether from their neighbors, businesses, or government officials. Similarly, members of marginalized secular groups such as those in the LGBTQ community may be harassed for what others perceive as "sinful" qualities related to whom they happen to love or what gender they happen to express.

Years may pass before the full scope of Congressional actions and these court decisions is known and how the resulting corruption of religious liberty may impact government funding for research and public health. Citizens who claim that it goes against their religious rights to support government funding of certain types of scientific research that utilize embryonic stem cells, such as research into cures for Parkinson's, Alzheimer's, and juvenile diabetes, could significantly jeopardize public health and science. Likewise, business owners who claim that the provision of certain medicines violates their sincerely held religious beliefs could jeopardize the health of their employees and cause a significant burden on the government to provide those resources in their stead. These exemptions from providing medicine and medical procedures could open the floodgates to corporate religious exemptions for other important medical procedures such as blood transfusions, immunizations, and psychiatric care.

Almost any medical procedure could be seen as violating the religious beliefs of one or more religious group or sect. On the other hand, conservative religious beliefs about the origin of personhood and end-of-life choices frequently come into conflict with rapidly changing medical capabilities. Adherents of the Church of Scientology, including many business owners, tend to oppose the use of psychiatry and many psychotropic medications and may, therefore, seek exemptions to being required to cover such treatment. A Christian Scientist employer might use a precedent set here to refuse to cover almost any medicine. Such exemptions could expand well beyond the health care arena and include corporate religious exemptions to discrimination, child labor and safety laws, and even Social Security taxes.

Unless a coalition of humanist and progressive allies can stop the advance of this attack on basic freedoms, this precedent may allow individuals, religious groups, and corporations to be exempt from any law or regulation that they suddenly find to be opposed to their religious teachings. If that happens, the door will be wide open to unabated legal religious imposition and discrimination.

Creating Our Own Light at the End of the Tunnel

In order to reverse this negative situation, we need to unite around our nontheism and dispel the prejudice it invokes in order to be seen as equals in our own society. On the legal front, we can take a page from the fight for same-sex marriage equality.

When cases were brought in various states that successfully argued for same-sex marriage, they were done in a particular way that has lessons to teach nontheists both in the legal realm and in the public debate. What was argued was that a prohibition on same-sex unions violated gay and lesbian couples' right to equal protection under the law as indicated in the state constitution.

There are two key elements here. First, the basis was the equal protection argument, which requires government to treat all people equally, without unfair discrimination—in this case, requiring that same-sex couples get the same protections as opposite-sex couples. The second key element of this success was the use of state courts, smartly steering clear of the dangerous waters of the federal courts. It was possible to keep the legal battle in the state because the case was brought under the state constitution's equal protection clause, which is unlikely to be appealable to a federal court. That two-pronged strategy led to major victories for same-sex marriage.

We can do the same thing seeking to protect the rights of humanists, atheists and other freethinkers. This seemingly obvious approach hasn't been tried before, perhaps because we didn't see ourselves as a united group worthy of equal protection. There's plenty of support for this concept in the case law.

The Supreme Court declared back in 1994, just as government cannot "segregate people on account of their race, so too it may not segregate on the basis of religion." They also said: "A government cannot be premised on the belief that all persons are created equal when it asserts that God prefers some."

The Establishment Clause/taxpayer standing dilemma is not the same kind of problem with equal protection cases. Proof of injury is satisfied by the unequal treatment itself because religious discrimination is presumptively unconstitutional, meaning the government would have to show a compelling reason for any unequal treatment. What needs to be proven is unequal treatment or discrimination against the person's group—in our case, nontheists.

This has an advantage over the old government sponsorship of religion cases. It presents our argument as direct discrimination against atheists and agnostics, not just a violation of an abstract principle. And the Religious Right loves to argue that religious monuments are historic and must be preserved, but the "It's historic!" argument won't work here because an historic pattern of discrimination just strengthens an equal protection case. Even swayable folks in the general public know it's wrong to treat some folks different as the religiously-biased monuments plainly do.

While the Religious Right is arguing that "separation of church and state" can't be found in the Constitution, we're looking to bring the struggle to the real issue before us, namely that discrimination and the prejudice that gives rise to it must be addressed head on. Atheist-humanist equality is worth fighting for, and by fighting for our rights we'll be protecting the rights of all Americans to believe, or not believe, as they see fit.

Combined with our legal efforts, educating the public is critical, as we found when polling around the issue of the Pledge of Allegiance.

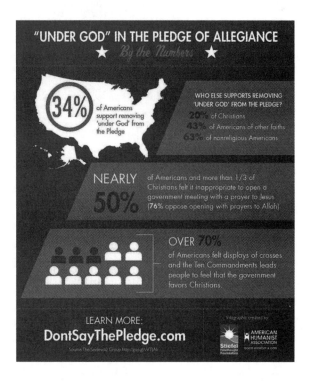

If we get past the prejudice so commonly faced by humanists and others who don't believe in a traditional god, what are the possibilities for the future?

CHAPTER 6

Past and Present Aspirations for a Better Future

Envisioning the future, we should strive for a world at peace where humanist values have become widely accepted as the basis for a global community that is tolerant, sensitive to environmental concerns, and respectful of diversity. To get there, a profound change in public opinion is needed, and thus humanists everywhere must emphasize advocacy in order to create the change we would like to realize.

Our Country's Founders

In thinking about the future, we benefit from reviewing the visions of those who came before. Sadly, a majority in this nation believe that it's a Christian nation and fail to take into consideration how the Founders demonstrated their lack of interest in identifying government with religious concepts by writing a fully secular constitution.

Despite the pervasiveness of the information and exhibits in museums like the Smithsonian, most Americans would be disturbed to even see a picture of a page from the Bible, torn out and all the supernatural words removed with scissors. If they heard it was at the hands of a government official, or even the president, cries would swiftly label it evidence of an atheist takeover or an all-out attack on Christianity. But of course, that's the "Jefferson Bible," what Thomas Jefferson compiled by rigorously editing six different Biblical texts into a concise book that was devoid of supernatural events. Even the crowning moment of the Christian story, Jesus' resurrection, is completely deleted from Jefferson's version. And of course, that's not all that contradicts the "Christian nation" myth.

I admit to some guilty pleasure at seeing faithful-looking families discover what the Jefferson Bible was really about when I saw them visiting the Smithsonian American History Museum while it was on display in 2012. Perhaps magnifying the shock for them was that the exhibit used Jefferson's title above the archway entrance "The Life and Morals of Jesus of Nazareth, by Thomas Jefferson." So uninformed folks would see that and think, "Here's the proof; we are a Christian nation!" that is, until they went inside.

Much has been made of the religious views of the Founders by pundits like Glenn Beck. These voices would have you believe that the Founders were devout believers who saw America as an inherently Christian nation. They point to the phrase in the Declaration of Independence, noting that people's natural rights are "endowed by their Creator" and the fact that many Founders cited God and Christianity in personal correspondence, some even offering religious invocations in public settings.

But the picture is more complicated than it would seem. The Founders shared little consensus on religion and engaged in sometimes acrimonious debate about the role of faith in public life and the role of God in human affairs. Benjamin Franklin and Thomas Paine were explicit deists. This term has come to mean a variety of things, from a cloaked atheism to a simple rejection of the Trinitarian view of Christianity. Franklin's private writings found him offering some doubts as to Jesus's divinity, with Franklin later coming to be called the "Prophet of Tolerance" for his embrace of many faiths. Thomas Paine's deism was explicitly anti-Christian, and it was his openness about his beliefs that put him at odds with many of the Founders. Indeed, Paine's *The Age of Reason* prompted such a vigorous debate amongst the founding set that even Jefferson argued against its publication, with Franklin condemning it. But Paine believed in a Creator and was at pains to say so whenever he was faced with the terrifying charge of "atheist."

This charge was also leveled at Presidents Jefferson and James Madison. A principal author of the Constitution and no friend to organized religion, Madison famously composed a "Detached Memoranda" decrying religious influence as injurious to public life. Attacking a proposal by Patrick Henry to have the state fund equally all Christian churches, Madison took aim at the history of organized Christianity:

> During almost fifteen centuries has the legal establishment of Christianity been on trial. What have been its fruits? More or less in all places, pride and indolence in the Clergy, ignorance and servility in the laity, in both, superstition, bigotry, and persecution.

And yet, as president, Madison issued Thanksgiving proclamations that explicitly praised God. Perhaps it was heartfelt, or perhaps Madison was caving to political pressure just as politicians do today. Think of all the members of Congress, including many closeted nonbelievers, who voted to add a prayer plaque to the secular World War II Memorial in Washington, DC.

On the more traditional and conservative side of religion and public life are figures like Patrick Henry and John Adams. Adams, apparently a fence-sitting Unitarian and occasional deist, responded violently to Paine's publication of *The Age of Reason*, offering a full throated defense of Christianity, calling it "above all the religions that ever prevailed or existed in ancient or modern times, the religion of wisdom, virtue, equity, and humanity." But while Adams sometimes praised the Ten Commandments and the Beatitudes in his private correspondence, he admitted to personal doubts—many scholars believe Adams, like Jefferson, did not recognize the divinity of Christ, regarding him rather as a significant moral teacher.

Patrick Henry, on the other hand, was a committed Christian—so much so that he believed his beloved wife Sarah suffered from long-term demonic possession. When she died, he refused to give her a Christian burial and instead had her interred thirty feet beneath the ground near his home. Henry also advocated staunchly for a religious tax to support an established state church in his home state of Virginia. This tax would be collected from all citizens, regardless of faith, but would then go toward the funding of the Christian church of their choice. This initiative is notable for several reasons—not just its support by George Washington, but also the fierce opposition it engendered in men like Jefferson and Madison. Jefferson's memoirs contain this passage on his Virginia Statute for Religious Freedom (legislation diametrically opposed to Henry's state-sponsored religious initiative):

> Where the preamble declares, that coercion is a departure from the plan of the holy author of our religion, an amendment was proposed by inserting "Jesus Christ," so that it would read, "A departure from the plan of Jesus Christ, the holy author of our religion;" the insertion was rejected by the great majority, in proof that they meant to comprehend, within the mantle of its protection, the Jew and the Gentile, the Christian and Mohammedan, the Hindoo and Infidel of every denomination.

Indeed, Jefferson's own religious views are as complex as the opinions of the Founders overall. There exist accounts of an elderly Jefferson expressing atheistic sentiments to a houseguest, but they are controversial at best. When Jefferson was accused of atheism in the presidential election of 1800, the charge stuck largely because Jefferson was even then famously skeptical. Writing to Benjamin Rush in the twilight of his years (likely while he was in the process of compiling the Jefferson Bible), he wrote, "To the corruptions of Christianity I am indeed opposed; but not to the genuine precepts of Jesus himself. I am a Christian, in the only sense he wished any one to be; sincerely attached to his doctrines, in preference to all others; ascribing to himself every human excellence; and believing he never claimed any other."

Jefferson's famous "Wall of Separation" letter to the Danbury Baptists, too, has been the subject of much controversy. Jefferson used the phrase in explaining to the Danbury Baptists that "Religion is a matter which lies solely between Man and his God..." and called the First Amendment "that act of the whole American people which declared that their legislature ... [was] building a wall of separation between Church and State." Yet uncertainty exists even in language as strong as this because Jefferson was referring to Congress when he used the term "their legislature," and Jefferson was a noted proponent of state's rights, going so far as to draft a separate statute on religious freedom in the state of Virginia. This has been interpreted by some to mean that Jefferson felt the federal government had no right to impose religious tests, but that perhaps states could. Indeed, the Bill of Rights was not considered applicable to the conduct of state governments until after the Civil War and the passage of the Fourteenth Amendment.

One thing is clear: the Founders did not hold one view on religion, even individually. Their writings reflect an open skepticism about religion and doubts about the existence of God. It's also impossible to separate them from their time. With a long lineage of bloody religious wars in England and continental Europe, the Founders likely saw America as an opportunity to start anew and build a community of tolerance. Even the devout Henry advocated for toleration of people of different denominations.

Knowing the history, it's clear that Christianity was not America's "founding religion." In fact, one of the first treaties ratified by the newly minted United States Senate explicitly disavowed Christianity as America's official religion. The Treaty of Tripoli, submitted and signed into law by John Adams, declared:

> As the Government of the United States of America is not, in any sense, founded on the Christian religion; as it has in itself no character of enmity against the laws, religion, or tranquility, of Mussulmen [Muslims]; and, as the said States never entered into any war, or act of hostility against any Mahometan nation, it is declared by the parties, that no pretext arising from religious opinions, shall ever produce an interruption of the harmony existing between the two countries.

During a time when a number of our nation's representatives spend hours on camera endorsing a near theocratic view of Christianity in America, the views of the Founders provide some much needed balance.

A Humanist Approach to Traditional Religions

After discussing the views of the founders, we are well-positioned to consider how humanists can best relate to traditionally religious people today. An overarching theme for this relates to respect being attached to people, not ideas.

As mentioned earlier, we must retain the ability to provide unfettered critique of ideas. It's essential to provide such criticism if we're to have progress toward more reasonable, defendable, reality-based decision-making. And religion is by no means beyond criticism, so we should feel free to discredit conclusions without evidence and even poke fun at the occasional absurdity. But when critique becomes belittling, when poking fun becomes ridiculing, the respect between people that is the foundation for any meaningful conversation is lost.

When talking with humanists I find that most see it as distasteful to publicly disparage religious people. Humanists seem to oppose hateful rhetoric naturally and understand that you can respectfully disagree with the viewpoints an individual may hold, but not respectfully ridicule the individuals themselves.

Just as crucial to our success as critique, is building the alliances we need in order to achieve our aims. As a minority group, we have to join with others if we're to prevail on matters of self-preservation and inclusion as well as with the individual forward-thinking positions humanists tend to hold. In order to build those alliances and to simply be good neighbors, it behooves us to not allow our understandable devaluation of traditional religious arguments to cloud our thinking and prejudice us against religious people. This is especially true when we consider religious minorities that are already experiencing prejudice and discrimination from a society that frequently favors its majority religion. So we should be on our guard against bigotry targeting Muslims, Jews, and others, and prevent prejudice from entering our thinking or influencing our communities. When we see that happening, it's our responsibility to speak out. By speaking out, we're not only doing the right thing, but we're also positioning ourselves to participate in alliances that we need in order to be successful.

I first heard the reference to the age old concept of short-term allegiances from Meg Riley, then the Director of the Washington Office for the Unitarian Universalist Association. During a press conference at the National Press Club in Washington DC, Riley said "We have no permanent friends and no permanent enemies in politics," explaining that the UUA would sometimes ally with unlikely partners in their efforts to support religious liberty. Humanists engage in such short-term alliances as well. If the Scientologists, Hindus, and Seventh Day Adventists will work with us to protect the freedom to think and believe as we see fit, why not ally with them on that issue? This is true even if we might disagree on the creation of religious exemptions to necessary rules or a whole host of other concerns.

Of course, there's a spectrum of likelihood that we'd agree and ally with any particular faith group. We've much more in common with the Quakers, Jews, and Buddhists than we do the Pentecostal Christians, Fundamentalist Mormons, and Islamist Muslims. Even within denominations there exist those more or less willing to work with humanists such as the moderate Cooperative Baptist Fellowship vs. the Southern Baptist Convention. Sometimes atheists and freethinkers unthinkingly lump all Christians or Muslims together as if billions of people can have monolithic views. By recognizing the true variety, we have the chance to ally with the more progressive elements and seek to nudge entire religions in a humanistic, atheist-friendly direction. Such a strategy will be far more effective than attempts at conversion.

A Way Forward

When envisioning the future it's worth reminding ourselves that such visioning is a creative exercise that's different for different people and itself evolves over time. As 2011 AHA Humanist of the Year Rebecca Newberger Goldstein wrote in *Plato at the Googleplex: Why Philosophy Won't Go Away*, "Humanity should never be frozen into a vision of the best. A creative society must be willing to tolerate some degree of instability because creativity is inherently unstable."

From Friedrich Nietzsche to Christopher Hitchens, many who were convinced of religion's negative impact falsely predicted its demise. Those whose worldviews are solidly built with a frame of logic and on the firm foundation of knowledge often forget that they are in the minority. After all, as of 2013, 29 percent of Americans still believe in astrology. Just because faith requires adherence to unproven and unprovable assertions does not mean that such ideas will be abandoned now, or even over time, by everyone. Much more likely is that the human need for resolution, the tendency to hold on to what's desired, and simple inertia will maintain spiritual faith at some level indefinitely.

While religion and spirituality may persist, it certainly will not be as it is today in the future—not ten years from now and not into more distant decades. Partly spurring this change is the nontheists who were spurred to action by the Religious Right ascendency into the American political sphere. They understand the need for social activism now in a way they didn't in previous decades.

History has seen the evolution of religion from tribal animisms and other polytheistic faiths to monotheistic ones. A few religions, including some modern schools of Buddhism, New Age worldviews, and religious philosophies are even in the realm of "post-theological."

One steady change we've seen is the lessening impact of traditional religion on richer societies. Where once religion held equal sway over political, social, and spiritual domains, we've seen that authority recede. Political authority is rarely granted today in the same way it was under Holy Roman emperors and the divine right of kings. Social control in the West is far less stringent than it once was, with the churches losing their hold on rules surrounding courting, marriage, and the family. Even mainline churches are seeing their domains shrinking as discoveries provide testable explanations for movements of the stars, the origins of species, and the birth of the universe. For some, these facts remove the need to rely on spirituality.

As we move into the future, one can predict where traditional spirituality will continue to lose its authority. The churches will eventually surrender their currently losing battles on gay marriage, on a woman's right to choose, and on the maintenance of stereotyped gender roles. But it will also lose in struggles that are just beginning. The prejudice seen commonly among the faithful today—that goodness can only come through godliness—will be less and less accepted. As more and more of the population who are atheists and agnostics come out of the closet to their friends, family, and neighbors, it will be difficult to hold to the claim that so many lack the ability to lead productive moral lives. As this claim breaks down, religion and spirituality will begin to lose its connection to goodness in general. No longer will it be a social liability to voice secular and rationalist principles.

Being part of secular humanist communities will be an accepted alternative to traditionally religious ones and preferred over increasingly irrelevant fundamentalist faiths. Fundamentalists will no longer get the support they need to impose religion in the military, the democratic process, and the schools. When the time comes to mark marriages, funerals, and the like, evocative and inspiring humanist ceremonies will become the norm for these life events because they address the needs of an increasingly diverse culture.

The scientific method, with its basis in observation, analysis, and experimentation, will be seen as the driving force for determining valid choices for public policy. People will understand that science is a way to seek answers, not something to "believe" in, and polls will show vast majorities accepting human evolution over creationism, supporting comprehensive sex education, and understanding how human intervention impacts our environment.

As politicians campaign for public office, the days when it was political suicide to be a humanist or an atheist will be long gone. Like President John F. Kennedy's efforts to show his political actions to be separate from the Catholic Church, future political leaders will go even further in trying to position their belief systems in humanistic terms. The increasingly less common religious candidates will admit that they believe in a higher power but stress that they base their decisions on the here and now.

This may not all come to pass by in the next decade, but progress should be clearly visible. Although Christianity and other religious traditions will remain, the writing will soon be on the wall for the end of Christian social and political dominance in the United States.

With all these changes occurring, what will the new spirituality look like? Perhaps the word itself will slip from usage since it's derived from something so debatable. When people say they are spiritual but not religious, as it is frequently heard, they often just mean that they're not robotic and unfeeling but embrace their emotional responses to the world and don't ignore intuitive impulses. After there's better language in common usage to communicate these feelings, the idea of shared values and a vision for a better future will remain.

Humanists will encourage empathy, along with the compassion and the sense of inherent equal worth that flow from it, in a way that honors human knowledge about ourselves and our universe. This means applying the scientific method to our pursuit of happiness and well-being, a pursuit we see as not just a solitary one but one for us to strive for as a society. When we look at the world in this way, we discover that improving oneself, nurturing others, and working to improve society are the keys to deep-seated happiness. Those ideals are consistent with many traditional morals: integrity, fidelity, and an independent work ethic.

And this unified, humanistic approach toward bettering our world will come to replace today's "interfaith" endeavors, since this is the true common core element driving collaborations labeled interfaith today. Such good works need not be limited to people of faith. While humanist approaches aren't yet often recognized as the commonality, this will be more frequently seen as preconceived negative ideas of humanism fade. Of course, people will no longer regard religious ideas as outside the realm of analysis and critique. Respect for the various gods and religions may diminish, but respect for parents, teachers, and others who've accumulated knowledge will increase. Unquestioned devotion to sacred days and places will diminish, just as appreciation for subject area expertise will increase. The finality of death will be a challenge for many to grapple with, but fear of the unknown will be replaced with an acceptance of uncertainty, greater curiosity, and joy for life.

So looking to the future, we see a changing landscape. Religious faith, with its assortment of positives and negatives, will persist. While mainstream faiths will remain part of our culture, traditional and fundamentalist religious ideas will recede. As their influence diminishes, rational, humanistic answers will come to occupy center stage.

But this vision of what may be isn't the automatic course of history. Too often, history has reminded us that trends in the right direction may suddenly reverse, be they reductions in anti-Semitism, reduced support for creationism, drops in anti-abortion fervor, or a myriad of other moves toward a more humanistic future. Fundamentalist backlashes against such gains need to be anticipated and prepared for.

In order for tomorrow to move in an enlightened direction humanists and nontheists of all stripes must unite coalitions on every matter facing us today. As Frederick Douglass said: "Power concedes nothing without a demand." Our rigorous actions are essential, and our efforts have to be so powerful that they inspire others of like mind to join us. It's only through such efforts that we can overcome those who aggressively seek to pull us backwards.

As the closing lines of *Humanism and Its Aspirations* state, "We aspire to this vision with the informed conviction that humanity has the ability to progress toward its highest ideals. The responsibility for our lives and the kind of world in which we live is ours and ours alone."

PART II

APPLICATIONS

"As indicated by our very name, we humanists celebrate humanity, want humanity to survive, and recognize that if humanity does survive, it will be by its own efforts. Never can we sit back and wait for miracles to save us. Miracles don't happen. Sweat happens. Effort happens. Thought happens. And it is up to us humanists to help—to expend our sweat, our effort, and our thought. Then there will be hope for the world."

-Isaac Asimov, in the September/October 1989
issue of the *Humanist* magazine

CHAPTER 7

Political Consequences
of Humanism

Herb Silverman is the founder of the Secular Coalition for America, a lobbying organization that represents the American Humanist Association, the American Ethical Union, the Society for Humanistic Judaism, and other collegial groups in the halls of Congress. Writing for the *Washington Post*, Herb said:

> Theist or nontheist, we are all evangelists for issues that matter to us. The question isn't whether we should proselytize, but how and how often? ... I think we shouldn't be screaming atheists, nor should we go door-to-door spreading the word that there are no gods. But many of us are comfortable writing letters to the editor, participating in forums or debates, writing to members of Congress, or coming out of our atheist and humanist closets at appropriate times. For all of us, religious or not, people are likely to respect our worldview more for what we do, than for what we preach.

When we think about Herb's approach toward outreach and activism, it's easy to see that something must be done if we're to raise the positive profile of our worldview. The call to civic responsibility on behalf of reason-based values has never been more sorely needed in America than it is today.

Religious Right leaders continue to get their supporters in federal and state governments to advance their extreme conservative, sectarian agenda. They are working publicly and behind the scenes to push the appointment of far right judges and regressive legislation, and they are also directly espousing their narrow religious views. The danger of the government's public embrace of religious belief is that it inhibits academic freedom, compromises civil liberties, and tears down the wall of separation between religion and government.

A new embrace of humanistic reason is needed to hold back this assault on our protections and prevent us from going down a path of theocratic despotism. Humanism provides a needed philosophical foundation. While humanism may not be dogmatic with unchangeable rules, there is general consensus among humanists about our approach to issues; some of these principles are laid out in *Humanism and its Aspirations*. Without cataloguing political positions, it frames the debate by highlighting the importance of human progress, human dignity, equality, global responsibility, civil liberties, secular society, the environment, and a commitment to science over blind faith and pseudoscience. This document also boldly asserts that we can resolve our differences without resorting to violence. Found in full in the appendices of this book, in summary, they are:

- Knowledge of the world is derived by observation, experimentation, and rational analysis;

- Humans are an integral part of nature, the result of unguided evolutionary change;

- Ethical values are derived from human need and interest as tested by experience;

- Life's fulfillment emerges from individual participation in the service of humane ideals;

- Humans are social by nature and find meaning in relationships;

- Working to benefit society maximizes individual happiness.

The first bullet goes to the point well covered in Part One related to using science and experience rather than ancient texts and divine revelation to determine knowledge. It also has an aside that values the arts and other aesthetic pursuits. Like the other parts of humanistic thought, this has real impact on active political questions being debated in the halls of power. If we accept scientific facts as a firmer basis for decision-making than faith, then the idea that the nation's history of religious fervor should be promoted as an honored accomplishment becomes ludicrous. God need not be referenced on money, in government buildings, or in our pledges of allegiance. And using religious dogma as support for political positions is automatically discarded. So faith opposition to equal rights for LGBTQ Americans dissolves, as does a religious basis for anti-abortion positions. Of course, it also impacts our support for unfettered scientific research.

The second bullet, "Humans are an integral part of nature, the result of unguided evolutionary change," is to some degree an extension of the first. It centers on how humanity's dependence on the same evolutionary processes that all other life forms are bound by—and it speaks to accepting the limits of our current knowledge. This forces us to recognize and respect nature and the animal kingdom of which we are part. It challenges the idea that public schools should be teaching religious alternatives to what we've learned explains our existence most convincingly. Being able to live with the understanding that some answers are not yet known, and that the answers we do have may undergo revision as we learn more, means that we don't need to accept arbitrary answers for unusual phenomena. Instead of seeing a weeping statue of the Virgin Mary as evidence of godly intervention, we remain skeptical of extraordinary claims and continue to pursue the truth. (A weeping Mary statue in Mumbai was actually caused by a leaky sewage pipe, as described in *The Guardian*.)

The third bullet, "Ethical values are derived from human need and interest as tested by experience," speaks to humanist ethics and morality—how they are fully this-world creations. It also hints at the priorities of humanists, such as the environment, as well as human and civil rights. Unlike conservative Christians who base their hopes for our world on prayers to a higher power and tend to reject evidence of humanity's impact on climate change, humanists see that there is no other force to which we can entrust our ecosystem other than ourselves. And humanists see that human and civil rights are inseparable from treating people with worth and dignity. Group-based discrimination isn't supportable as an ethical stance in humanism, whether it's based in gender, ethnicity, sexuality, or a number of other bases. For humanists, acting out of prejudice is unethical.

The fourth bullet, "Life's fulfillment emerges from individual participation in the service of humane ideals," relates to human sources for meaning and happiness, and speaks to the purpose that past AHA honorary president Kurt Vonnegut spoke of when he explained why he was a humanist. For him, and many others, being a humanist means seeking to better oneself and society, and enjoying the experience along the way. By taking the view that life's challenges, as difficult as they may be, eventually can become opportunities for growth, we are also motivated to learn about history and keep its lessons in the forefront of our minds as we confront the present. This is why humanist writers like Howard Zinn, Jared Diamond, and Barbara Ehrenreich are reminding us of how humanity's past experiences shouldn't be forgotten as we head into the future.

The fifth bullet, "Humans are social by nature and find meaning in relationships," draws on our recognition of the importance of our relationships in providing personal fulfillment. I've seen a number of surveys incorrectly conclude that religion is a physically and mentally healthy choice, but just as Philip Moeller suggested in his article about this phenomenon, it has more to do with social networking with the like-minded than it does with religion. Surveys mistakenly compare socially inactive atheists with socially active faithful and jump to conclusions. What's increasingly recognized is that having the support of loved ones and a community is a healthier alternative than going it alone. In order to build more robust communities at the local and the societal levels, we have to find meaning in relationships.

Those with strong social networks are less likely to resort to violence. Realizing this fact inspires humanist commitments to a sound justice system free from bias. It supports the value of rehabilitation, and suggests the need to encourage moral behavior. We can also acknowledge that the ready availability of violent weapons correlates with violent crime, and so we endeavor to balance conflicting values of individual liberty with that which is best for everyone. We can see evidence of this balance in the humanist support of assault weapon bans, waiting periods, and background checks for gun owners, but hesitating to endorse an outright ban on firearms, which would excessively compromise individual liberties.

The sixth bullet, "Working to benefit society maximizes individual happiness," reminds us that benefiting others is a way to help ourselves. It also highlights the importance of building community on a global scale, doing what we can to raise the standards of living for all people. Part of this is recognition that rampant inequality is cancerous to our world. Extremes of wealth and poverty, of cosmopolitanism and ignorance, are the seeds of conflict and instability. When the bulk of a society has no hope of achieving the basic standards of life and happiness, it cultivates religious extremism and opens the door to violence as coping methods for the disenfranchised. Humanists seek to do what we can to help by supporting the United Nations Millennium Goals related to eradicating poverty and hunger, achieving universal primary education, promoting gender equality, reducing child mortality, improving maternal health, fighting disease, ensuring environmental sustainability and developing a global partnership. And humanists have long supported the United Nations Declaration on Human Rights, which strives to detail the inherent rights human beings hold—from basic health to freedom of religion and conscience. While well-meaning humanists may disagree on some details in broad statements like these, being involved prevents us from taking an isolationist perspective and allows us to consider international involvement in the light of what might be best for humanity.

Open to Review, But Not Apolitical

In light of the above, it's evident that while humanist positions aren't dogmatic, they're by no means apolitical and exhibit a tendency toward liberalism. Exploring the numbers, there are indeed very few humanists who call themselves "conservative" in the general sense. In the last survey of American Humanist Association members, less than three percent claimed to be members of the Republican Party, and of that small number, many are aiming to reform Republicanism to be more socially liberal than it is today. Exploring the issues touched on above, and those to follow, and then comparing those positions to that found in the Republican Party platform, it all makes very good sense.

Certainly, it's possible to hold conservative views about one of a number of issues, especially when competing values are at stake. I know of dedicated humanists who seem to emphasize liberty over anti-violence measures when they express their strong interest in maintaining the ability to buy, own, and carry guns. But those same folks tend not to be extreme in their view and are willing to accept waiting periods for gun purchases, mandatory registrations and limitations on the right to carry them in various places as ways to accommodate their values without facilitating violence. Similarly, I know humanists who believe that the freedom to die can be precarious in its application, endangering those who are going through a mentally difficult time, and exposing infirm people to risk of manipulation. But such individuals also tend to see their position in moderation, frequently agreeing with Oregon's Death with Dignity laws that include safeguards confining use to terminally ill patients with doctor-certified control of their mental capacities. In general, I've found that humanists who describe their politics as "conservative" aren't anywhere near as conservative as average Republicans and their often religiously motivated staff members that I've interacted with on Capitol Hill.

We also have members, though only one to two percent, who identify as libertarian, believing that people (and often businesses) should be allowed to do what they like without government inter-ference. The home of the extreme right-wing Tea Party, libertarian-ism isn't immediately recognizable as having anything humanist about it, but there are issues where the Libertarian Party platform and humanism coincide. Both support keeping government out of abortion and other reproductive rights questions, both condemn ethnic, sexuality, age, and belief-based bigotry, and both tend to be reluctant to use military force. Personally, I find libertarianism's reliance on self-policing and rejecting the potential of using gov-ernment power for good to be theories that just don't provide the best results in practice, but others are free to disagree. The human-ists I know who are attracted to the theories behind libertarianism tend to "lean libertarian" rather than be strong advocates of ac-cepting the ideology whole cloth.

It's not automatically inconsistent with humanism to reach the rational conclusion that local government is often preferable to federal government, that the private sector can do a number of things better than the public sector, that we shouldn't be burden-ing our grandchildren with debt, or that the cost/benefit ratio of some government regulations is out of whack. If folks arrive at a traditionally conservative position through genuine reason and compassion, rather than through dogma and selfishness, not only are they still humanist, but they may have discovered knowledge about a situation that's eluded others.

There are topics that are commonly grounds for debate in humanist circles. While some humanists would emphasize the need to challenge and even legally limit pornography because of the industry's negative impact on women, other humanists (possi-bly in greater numbers, based on anecdotal evidence) want to limit or remove restrictions on pornography because they consider it a freedom of speech issue, even potentially healthy for sexual expres-sion. Similarly balancing free expression and oppression, many humanists are on both sides of the debate regarding France's ban on wearing the burqa in public and the extent to which it's accept-able or not for people in the West to be critical of Muslims. There's even a large minority of humanists who directly tie their humanism to their commitments to animal rights and vegetarianism or veganism.

Regardless of individual differences, humanists of all stripes recognize that we need to work together to make things better because no deity is going to do it for us. While we humanists don't agree among ourselves on everything, and we may even change our minds from time to time, we have the insight to see that this can be our strength, not our weakness! We know we need to work together because a form of religious fundamentalism has emerged and gained ground across the country that is both anti-secular and political, and it's a danger to the democracy and values we humanists hold dear.

As mentioned earlier, but bears repeating because the words still apply so strongly today, Frederick Douglass said: "Power concedes nothing without a demand." Though we've seen important changes in who holds offices on Capitol Hill and outside Washington, DC, those elected are confronted by a still-powerful fundamentalist right and a pervasive sense that they can't remain successful without pandering to religious conservatives. That's why we continue to see more faith-based initiatives, new efforts to establish fetal personhood, and opposition to treating same-sex couples equally. While Americans see this happening all too regularly on the home front, there are also similar and frequently more severe challenges abroad, a few that will be highlighted in the last part of this chapter.

Coming Out

Once you've moved beyond the restraints of a traditional god that intervenes in daily life to grant us favors or punish us, the next big consideration is when, where, and to whom to "come out" in that regard.

Take a moment and think about what it would be like to be a nontheistic teenager raised in an evangelical household. As someone who rejects divine revelation and outmoded texts as sources for truth, you are convinced your family's faith is based on nothing more than wishful thinking. Yet you wake up every Sunday, put on your best clothes, and go to worship with your family and community. Every word of praise to God you sing is a lie; every "Hallelujah" you utter is deception. And when you return home and fold your hands to pray for grace over dinner, you close your eyes and don't believe a word of it. Think about the fear you'd carry inside, the fear of being discovered, the fear of being outed. This same challenge exists for nontheists in fundamentalist Mormon or Muslim communities where the risk may be just as great or greater.

Some people view this sort of secrecy as timidity, but in fundamentalist communities, leaving the church, temple, or mosque is the greatest sin of all. It means having to start life all over again, but possibly this time, without your parents, your best friends, or any means of financial support. Every day, people are readily shunned and disowned for lesser sins than unbelief. If you faced this choice, would you speak out?

The distressing truth is that some of you *do* face decisions analogous to this one. You might be wrestling with secrecy every day, but you can't imagine being completely open about it because to do so would mean strains on your family, limitations on your career, or the end of important friendships. You already may have resolved never to speak about what you really think. There may be others reading this right now, thinking, "Why would I *ever* choose to come out as nontheist, if it means such terrible consequences?"

And for those in less hostile environments, coming out as a non-believer could still lead to rejection from someone close to you, such as a parent or friend. And if this is the case you may need to grieve the loss before you can comfortably get past this abandonment. But then consider how true, how committed, the relationship really was—and whether, ultimately, its value was commensurate to your personal integrity. Similar to a divorce (and it is a kind of divorce), the process of letting go can be challenging. But in time you'll probably feel that it was worth it.

It might not be easy, but as the AHA's 2013 Humanist of the Year Dan Savage promotes, "It gets better."

In recent decades, the LGBTQ rights movement has made great strides toward giving voice to millions of lesbian, gay, bisexual, and transgender people who have historically been severely silenced by prejudice and discrimination. Harvey Milk and other great pioneers of the movement were faced with harrowing retribution for their advocacy. They fought not only the threat of excommunication from their respective communities, but violence, legal sanctions, jail, and worse. But those men and women who stepped out of the darkness of stigmatization and shame, refusing to hide their hearts and minds, found that in time they were part of communities even more vibrant and satisfying than those they left behind.

If your loved ones refuse to believe that you can be a good person and a humanist, they have a prejudice that you might help them overcome by coming out. It might seem like the closet of belief is tolerable, but someday you might decide that it's better to live a life unconcealed, whether it's regarding sexuality, gender, or religious belief. Even if living a double life were possible, the cost is too high. Consider the energy it takes to suppress natural objections, attend services you don't support, revere a deity you don't believe in, and placate family and friends from whom you are in hiding. This silent suffering isn't necessary.

There are good and joyful reasons for being an open nontheist. I don't just mean sleeping in on Sundays or freeing up your Friday nights. There are many stories of children coming out to their church-going parents only to find that one or both of them are humanists, too! Millions of ostensible believers are, in fact, doubters, skeptics, and humanists. We are everywhere: from former Congressman Barney Frank to actors like Brad Pitt, Angelina Jolie, and Natalie Portman to *South Park* creators Trey Parker and Matt Stone to authors like Joyce Carol Oates and Sarah Vowell to musicians like Eddie Vedder and Kim Deal to comedians like Aziz Ansari and Ricky Gervais. Mark Zuckerberg, the co-founder of Facebook, also doesn't believe in a god. The list goes on and on, and is longer than we will ever know because of those too afraid to speak their mind. But you'll be more likely to know who in your community shares your feelings when you state them yourself. You might be pleasantly surprised how others react.

Then there's the indescribable happiness and relief of an out and open life. When you no longer need to feign an identity that isn't yours, you'll discover confidence and the ability to say, "This is who I am," and speak out on any issue that stirs your heart and mind. By announcing your presence, others will come out to you who you didn't previously know shared your nontheism. You'll finally be able to meet other nontheists and build relationships based on truth and honesty. You can love and be loved by people who know *the real you*. No matter what you've been told, that person deserves to see the light of day.

We're by no means the first to face this kind of challenge. In 1978, Proposition 6 was the failed California ballot measure aimed at preventing gay people from working as teachers in public schools. On election night that year, Harvey Milk said the following:

> ...to the gay community all over this state, my message to you is: so far a lot of people joined us and rejected Proposition 6, and we owe them something.
>
> We owe them to continue the education campaign that took place. We must destroy the myths once and for all, shatter them. We must continue to speak out, and most importantly, most importantly, every gay person must come out. As difficult as it is, you must tell your immediate family, you must tell your relatives, you must tell your friends, if indeed they are your friends, you must tell your neighbors, you must tell the people you work with, you must tell the people in the stores you shop in, and once they realize that we are indeed their children, that we are indeed everywhere, every myth, every lie, every innuendo will be destroyed once and for all.
>
> And once you do, you will feel so much better.

We must also come out as humanists, clearly stating that we don't rely on a higher power to govern our lives. When you and I come out, when elected officials come out, when celebrities like George Clooney come out, when any nontheist performs a public function well, it disproves the common myths that fuel prejudice against all of us.

We must educate the theist majority with evidence that humanists exist all around us, and the negative stereotypes have no basis whatsoever. Let's continue to grow the humanist movement, for ourselves, for our allies, and for all of humanity. Let's organize communities that further bring us together and give us confidence. Let's use that confidence to come out as nontheists and humanists and stand up for positive change.

International Humanism

As our species expanded to inhabit the world, our social structure evolved in a direction that contained increasing humanist potential. Beginning in extended family clans, and then further extended tribes, humanity gathered into agrarian communities, then city-states, then nations. In recent times, the concept of multinational governments such as the European Union is becoming the next stage. This trend is a humanistic one because it's an ever widening of the circle of "us" and a constantly shrinking circle of "them." If this life is all we have, it's no longer ethical to allow millions to suffer without our assistance. Even as, we personally explore ways of making our lives better, we ought to be devoting ourselves to making conditions better for others. When we realize that all humanity, in harmony with our environment, is the true "us," we can achieve humanistic progress not before contemplated.

Earlier chapters touched on the AHA's founding and continued involvement in the International Humanist and Ethical Union (IHEU) and, as just emphasized, the philosophy takes a clear one-world-one-people approach that acknowledges our common humanity. The world could benefit greatly from an approach like humanism that eschews various forms of divisive tribalism. In this twenty-first century, countries can no longer function securely and healthily in isolation from the rest of the world, and humanism can form the basis for mutual cooperation. That's why organized humanists at the AHA, the IHEU, and around the globe are supporting international religious freedom efforts and organizational cooperation through entities like the United Nations, the International Criminal Court, the World Health Organization, and others aiming to use our combined resources to make the world better.

Article Eighteen of the Universal Declaration of Human Rights states that "Everyone has the right to freedom of thought, conscience and religion; this right includes freedom to change his religion or belief, and freedom, either alone or in community with others and in public or private, to manifest his religion or belief in teaching, practice, worship and observance."

With the help of a newfound ally in the US State Department's Office of International Religious Freedom (IRF), the AHA increased its involvement on the international front by becoming a go-between with US government officials and nontheists globally. The AHA participated regularly with the Roundtable for Religious Freedom, the US Commission on International Religious Freedom (USCIRF), and other key entities. Such interactions opened the door for the creation of the Freedom of Thought Report, compiled and published by IHEU, which annually catalogs discrimination against atheists, humanists and the nonreligious worldwide.

Providing this report to the IRF office gave those involved the necessary information and inclination to add nontheist discrimination to the IRF's own reporting. The IRF's Annual Report to Congress on International Religious Freedom is a significant factor the US government considers in applying sanctions to nations and in other forms of international diplomacy. And the IHEU took the lead in getting their report in the hands of other nations' leadership as well.

Perhaps it's self-evident why international humanist activism for the nontheistic community is needed, but a few examples reinforce it.

Alexander Aan was in Indonesia, where only six official religions are recognized: Islam (representing 87 percent of the population), Protestantism, Catholicism, Hinduism, Buddhism and Confucianism. The law requires that all citizens hold an identification card that identifies them as one of the six religions, and atheism and agnosticism are not recognized. Blasphemy is illegal, carrying a five-year minimum jail sentence for those convicted. Alexander posted on his Facebook page simply the words, "God does not exist," and the next day was arrested at work and beaten by police. He was later sentenced to thirty months in prison for the crime of "inciting religious hatred or hostility." Muslim extremists have called for Aan to be beheaded.

A similar case affected an Egyptian named Alber Saber. He was raised a Christian but for the last ten years considered himself an atheist. In August of 2012 he shared a YouTube trailer for the anti-Islam film *Innocence of Muslims* on his Facebook page. The next month, a large protest took place at the U.S. Embassy in Cairo against the film. The day after the protest, Alber's home was surrounded by a mob calling for his death and threatening to burn down his house. When Alber's mother called the police, they didn't show up for two hours—and then they arrested Alber rather than the rioters. Alber was sentenced to three years in prison, where he was beaten. After he was released temporarily on appeal, he escaped from Egypt to an undisclosed location for safety reasons.

On January 7, 2015, the magazine office of *Charlie Hebdo* in Paris was the target of a coordinated attack where a dozen people were killed because of a perceived slight against the killers' religion of Islam. The atheistic magazine was critical of all religions, but it was its cartoons critical of Mohammad that apparently inflamed the killers to violence. Humanists led a worldwide outcry against this violent attempt to censor free speech. Author Salman Rushdie encapsulated the aim of many in his remarks: "I stand with *Charlie Hebdo*, as we all must, to defend the art of satire, which has always been a force for liberty and against tyranny, dishonesty, and stupidity."

With unfortunately many more examples like those above, it's all too clear that key issues of the current century will be how we handle the widespread negative impacts of fundamentalist thinking as well as how we navigate the waters between science and religion. As David Niose said in *Nonbeliever Nation: The Rise of Secular Americans*: "Breakthrough progress is possible on the one hand, and unthinkable disaster on the other." There's no doubt that we need to work together to make a difference globally. Socrates said he was "not an Athenian or Greek, but a citizen of the world." Being a global citizen is an important part of what it means to be a humanist.

While humanism is a constantly evolving philosophy that attempts to build on what we know to reach new heights of understanding, we're also ready to reconsider previously accepted notions, as evidence may undermine our past support of them. In this way, divergent views are not only accepted within humanism, they are encouraged. Exploring some examples in greater detail will help demonstrate how humanism is connected to day-to-day issues.

CHAPTER 8

Core Humanist Issues

Our knowledge of the world is constantly changing, and we benefit from remaining open minded and suspending judgment about matters which have multiple interpretations. Even though *how* we believe is more fundamental to humanism than *what* we believe, that doesn't mean that we can't find consensus about what makes sense based on our humanist convictions and what we see happening in the world around us.

Humanists seek to avoid over-generalizations, demagoguery that appeals to fear, and arguments not based on credible evidence. Instead, we seek to consider the impact policies will have on real people. When we don't have the information needed to accurately predict the consequences of our decisions we're often better off withholding judgment rather than jumping to conclusions. Challenges that societies and humanity face are different in different ages and locations. Today the core humanist issues relate to human rights, scientific integrity, and the rights and liberties that flow from them. Under that umbrella are found civil rights for ethnic minorities, LGBTQ rights, women's rights, secular government, promoting peace, reproductive freedoms and more.

Civil Rights

At the root of civil rights is one's ability to participate in society without being subject to discrimination. All Americans are entitled to the inalienable rights laid out in the US Constitution, not to be diminished by the government under any circumstances. This affects many groups in society and is perhaps exemplified in the struggle for racial equality.

Prejudice, such as that relating race to inherent criminality, is simply unsupported by the facts, meaning that it persists due to unchallenged ignorance. And like most bigotry this prejudice is unnatural—human beings aren't born racist or xenophobic. A quick view of diverse preschools, like the ones my daughters attended in the Washington DC area, reveals just how well kids get along without regard to ethnic and social divisions—that is, until they learn otherwise from their elders. This ignorance-based prejudice doesn't arise from nothing, but is taught by the previous generation and frequently accepted (just like faith) without evidence by those that follow. This tradition of generational prejudice is detrimental—even dangerous—for society because it leads to social strife and violence.

When prejudice is embedded in a new generation, it brands whole groups in society negatively, painting them as the outside "other" to be distrusted or feared. We've seen far too many examples of the impact this prejudice can have. A 2011 study for *American Economic Review* showed a clear racial bias in capital sentencing. And, as exemplified in Ferguson, Missouri, the fear that derives from racial prejudice spawns discriminatory behavior that can turn deadly.

The killing of Michael Brown on August 9, 2014, is a brutal reminder why traditions of all sorts, but especially those based in bigotry, mustn't be unconsciously passed down to children and reinforced with peers. Anything initially accepted on faith should be reconsidered, and we can reject those traditions based on prejudice or needless exclusion. This isn't an easy matter of choosing from a menu of options: rather it requires daily vigilance to prevent the blindness of the past from infecting how we treat people in the present. As Chris Mooney reveals in his article, "The Science of Why Cops Shoot Young Black Men," published in *Mother Jones*, discrimination is something often acted out unconsciously by well-meaning people.

It's not just about rejecting bad behavior either, since we also need to encourage the best traditions of humanity—the ones that help us learn empathy and act altruistically. While some have pointed to religion as an example of overcoming hate and moving toward equality, the evidence of historic religious support of slavery and apartheid suggests otherwise.

Traditions based in discrimination and prejudice need not persist indefinitely, for the unnatural byproducts of ignorance and scarcity can be overcome. Humanity has a history of an ever widening circle of what we mean when we say "us." Our notion of in-group has gone from extended families to tribes to city-states to nations to entities like the European Union. The time may come when we view humanity itself as the in-group that matters most. When we're no longer blinded by ignorance about ourselves and our world, but are instead better educated about nature and humanity, we'll see that prejudice has no place in our world. But as much as we might benefit by striving toward it, that utopian ideal isn't going to happen anytime soon, and we need to be prepared to deal with what people really think and do today if we're going to stop violence like that seen in Ferguson.

Prejudice, and the discrimination that results from it, must be fought at every turn. We must dispel ignorance with clear facts and living examples. We must shame those who would allow fear to reign and withhold any social acceptance for their discrimination. Those who engage in such acts must be consistently and appropriately dealt with; if they break a law, our justice system must ensure they don't go unpunished. If their discriminatory actions fall short of an illegal behavior, they could still be punished by society, where family and friends don't excuse it, but instead demonstrate the negative social consequences for such actions.

Respect for civil rights of all people is necessary for preserving the dignity of individuals and of humanity. If we can help or compel those who hold on to these morally bankrupt traditions to free themselves from such hateful ideas, the world can begin to heal itself of the damage caused over the years. When that time comes, the Michael Browns of the world will finally be able to walk the streets without an undue fear for their safety, and humanity as a whole will benefit.

Women's Rights

"If you say, 'I'm for equal pay,' that's reform. But if you say, 'I'm a feminist,' that's a transformation of society."
–Gloria Steinem

A discussion on challenging sexism and promoting women's rights through humanism starts with getting our own house in order as a prerequisite for further advancement of our aims. Atheism isn't immune from the influences of the broader culture, so atheists and humanists experience the effects of online hostility to women as well as face-to-face sexism at freethought conferences and other gatherings. Organizations and individuals have to take this into account in order to live by our own words.

It's also worth taking a moment to realize that humanists have an honorable feminist legacy, and that the feminist movements themselves were in fact led by a majority of humanists who set aside patriarchal religions in order to seek equality for all. Most folks have a sense today that humanism has historically supported feminism, but few realize how deep that connection is. Elizabeth Cady Stanton was a critic of traditional Christianity who wrote *The Women's Bible* and was the principal organizer of the Seneca Falls Convention in 1848, generally seen as the birthplace of feminism. And the American Humanist Association's involvement in feminism began almost as soon as it was founded.

From the AHA's early and active effort of elective abortion several decades ago, to our steadfast support to pass the Equal Rights Amendment (ERA), to our leadership in degenderizing publications, humanism was regularly ahead of the curve. Women's rights continue to be among our top priorities today. Past AHA President Bette Chambers said: "The AHA always recognized men and women as equals in all matters and has always been 'feminist.'" As discussed in the history of humanism section, the AHA awarded a veritable who's who in feminism over the years, from Margaret Sanger's activism in the early part of the twentieth century to Jessica Valenti's modern feminist advocacy today.

The current AHA board, where women make up seven of the twelve voting positions, has woman leadership in three of the four executive committee positions with President Rebecca Hale, Vice President Jennifer Kalmanson, and Secretary Susan Sackett.

But all the advocacy we can manage is needed to confront the Religious Right's and their allies' "war on women." Bills are regularly introduced by religious political extremists in Congress and the states to defund reproductive health services, elevate the rights of a fetus over that of women, repeal equal pay legislation, and more. In this modern era one might think that any form of gender prejudice or discrimination would be widely rejected. However, in addition to the new attacks on women's rights, pay inequity and other forms of institutionalized discrimination continue to plague women who are often relegated to second-class status by employers. Now that the basic health requirements of women are also under attack, it is essential to step up and guarantee the equality of women in America once and for all.

Looking at contraceptive care reveals what the Religious Right is capable of in the war on women. Contraception is something with extremely high support in the United States. Only the strictest of religious conservatives—Catholic, fundamentalist, or otherwise—would even suggest removing access to it. Yet their campaigns to do so have been unstoppable. When the Department of Health and Human Services required all businesses, including those affiliated with religious organizations, to provide contraceptive care to their employees, the opposition of national religious groups like the United States Conference of Catholic Bishops caused the Obama administration to compromise by delaying this rule for a year. Now, a result of the backward *Hobby Lobby* decision from the Supreme Court, which rests on the special rights for religion given by the Religious Freedom Restoration Act, companies can refuse to provide employees contraceptive care at all.

If America wishes to serve as an international example of liberty and just governance, we must ensure that all citizens are afforded the same rights and that institutionalized discrimination is made illegal. We must all come together, regardless of religious beliefs or political opinions, in order to guarantee equal treatment under the law and the end to gender discrimination.

On an optimistic note, according to a Barna study on religion, women are fleeing from traditional religion in record numbers. While women remain more religious than men overall, women's attendance in church has sunk by eleven percentage points since 1991, Bible reading plummeted by ten percentage points, and Sunday school involvement is down seven points. The number of women who are "unchurched" has risen seventeen percentage points—that's now more than half of American women who haven't attended church in the last six months. Shedding the shackles of gender discrimination in religion is a step in the right direction.

Today there are many fronts in this struggle that humanists are leading in favor of civil rights and against the war on women. Not only is it necessary to support the ERA, the Violence Against Women Act, and other positive efforts to level the playing field, we should also vigorously challenge Religious Right groups and their intellectual offspring, who are on the offensive regarding discrimination against women.

This war on women really is a battle over values. When the Religious Right advocates for "traditional values" related to women, what they mean is that their scriptures are more important than the health or rights of women nationwide. Humanists, freethinkers, and progressive people of faith, on the other hand, value Americans' right to necessary health services and value open and non-discriminatory workplaces instead.

LGBTQ Equality

Humanists understand that the constitutional guarantee of equal protection is supposed to be applied to all and advocate for marriage equality, employment non-discrimination, adoption rights, welcoming schools, and equal benefits for LGBTQ people. Today, same-sex couples are experiencing a special moment in history. With recognition of same-sex marriage it's clear that our work, along with that of other progressives, is making real change occur.

But as it was in California during the 2008 Proposition 8 debate, in the District of Columbia, and elsewhere, it's crystal clear that some faith-based groups are on the wrong side of history. It's not just the Religious Right either, as so-called mainstream religious organizations are trying to hold us back. Specifically, Catholic Charities has determined that maintaining a policy of discrimination is more important than doing good works when they abandoned their multi-million dollar adoption and foster care programs in DC and Illinois in anticipation of having to treat same-sex couples the same as heterosexual couples. But not only is Catholic Charities more concerned about the sexual preferences of potential parents than the well-being of the children they might raise, they also began a last ditch effort to rejigger their benefits package in order to skirt the law.

The Catholic Church's stance here highlights its continued unsuccessful efforts to cling to the past. Just as the church supported slavery for centuries, before finally bending to the weight of popular opinion, it will eventually be forced to give in to public pressure on same-sex relationships as well. Traditional religions that hold to divine revelations of ancient men and millennia-old texts are bound to be antiquated compared to the humanist drive to seek progress for humanity based on the best available evidence and reasoning.

What's clear today is that arguments for LGBTQ discrimination are based not upon considerations of public health or child success rates. Arguments along those lines used to be made based on biased and dated studies but, since they are so hopelessly flawed, you rarely see such efforts today. Instead, the anti-LGBTQ case is based purely on religiously enshrined prejudice. It's embarrassing and unjust that practices like employment or housing discrimination based on sexual orientation or gender identity persist in many states. One of the ways this discrimination continues is through fabricated debate on topics not worthy of deliberation.

Leading the opposition are religious fundamentalists, who interpret their holy scriptures as condemning homosexuality. While there are certainly two different opinions on LGBTQ equality, only one is a valid expression of political thought, while the other is merely a vocalization of deeply held bias.

Unlike the conversation about the national debt, where advocates argue in favor of or in opposition to austerity measures based upon economic models and rational considerations, the fight for LGBTQ rights is instead a battle between those with considered viewpoints on one side and those who express their personal and group intolerance on the other. Unfortunately, instead of ignoring hateful fundamentalist rants, the media reports on such issues as if both sides make an equally reasonable and compelling argument. The media often amplifies the stereotypes and other debasements in an effort to provide false balance to civil rights activists. Cenk Uygur, host of *The Young Turks* and recipient of the 2012 Humanist Media Award, explained at the American Humanist Association's annual conference that this problem is the result of a media that cares more about being perceived as "fair" by viewers than discerning the actual truth of an issue.

Everyone has a right to say what they believe, but people shouldn't expect to be taken seriously if what they say is so obviously based upon anti-gay prejudice. That's why humanists are happy to take part in advocating for full inclusion and equality.

Environment and Population Dynamics

During my first camping trip hiking along the Appalachian Trail alone, I entered a clearing and came upon a family of eagles flying just above me. The sereneness of my surroundings and the majesty of the eagles filled me with a sense of awe and wonder. I'm always thrilled at finding untouched spaces and exploring the life that thrives on our planet. But it seems more and more that such places are hard to find.

Certainly, humanity benefited over the past century from technological innovations and societal changes that have allowed us to reduce infant mortality and live longer, healthier lives than ever before. But this is not without its consequences as the planet and governments around the world struggle to deal with a rapidly growing global population.

Rampant pollution, food shortages, and conflict over increasingly scarce resources rise unabated. Our planet's ecosystem is hardly infinite in its resources to supply us what we need to sustain life or withstand our heedless actions that continue to degrade it. In fact, according to the World Wildlife Fund, humankind is already overusing the renewable resource capacity of Earth's biosphere by 50 percent. As more of our children survive infancy, something that wasn't guaranteed less than a century ago, and develop into adults who drive vehicles, eat livestock and crops, and have large families of their own due to a lack of family planning resources, this planet will suffer. And we're finding that things like food, jobs, and education aren't guaranteed.

As climate change and other environmental issues gain attention across the country and around the globe, it's worth remembering the words of *Humanism and Its Aspirations* that remind us of our "planetary duty to protect nature's integrity, diversity, and beauty in a secure, sustainable manner." The humanist commitment to the environment didn't start with that statement either—it was prominent in its predecessor document decades earlier, which read: "In learning to apply the scientific method to nature and human life, we have opened the door to ecological damage, over-population, dehumanizing institutions, totalitarian repression, and nuclear and bio-chemical disaster. Faced with apocalyptic prophesies and doomsday scenarios, many flee in despair from reason and embrace irrational cults and theologies of withdrawal and retreat." Humanist-minded environmentalists from Rachel Carson to Lester R. Brown confront these challenges instead of fleeing from them.

This is why it's so important to support the efforts of governments and private organizations that seek to promote family planning and help people to cooperatively decide to reduce population growth and live sustainable lifestyles. Programs, for example, that seek to educate us about—and prevent—food waste, or to broadly distribute contraception, help to combat environmental degradation, which is absolutely crucial if our children are to live in a world that can support them. The United Nations recognized this need for action in a recent report, which stated: "We must act now to halt the alarming pace of climate change and environmental degradation, which pose unprecedented threats to humanity."

Humanists hold a strong conviction that every human being is born with inherent dignity and the right to a life free from unnecessary pain and suffering. That sense of humanitarianism, combined with humanism's emphasis on scientifically accurate information and the role of technology in improving our quality of life, leads to a powerful support for family planning and other efforts meant to address the problems we face today.

Contraception is a key aspect of family planning, vital in poorer countries, since families there often struggle to feed, clothe, and shelter their children. Education must play a central role in these programs to ensure their overall effectiveness, and there's a special need to educate young girls and women. Several studies correlate such education with decreasing unwanted pregnancies as well as decreasing the rate of poverty. While some religious groups refuse to participate in comprehensive family planning efforts and claim that the distribution of contraceptives is immoral, or even evil, humanists see it as a means by which individuals can gain autonomy over their bodies, better plan for their future, and lead happier lives.

Thankfully, some religious folks also appreciate the need to act as good stewards of what they see as creation. It's a good thing they feel this way, or we wouldn't have the critical mass to effect necessary change. The AHA's 1999 Humanist of the Year, E. O. Wilson, was on the right track when he wrote *The Creation: An Appeal to Save the Earth*, which calls for science and religious leaders and individuals to set aside their differences to save the environment. Only together can we address the challenges before us and support a framework that will allow generations to come to live and thrive.

At the end of the day, these population dynamics and their consequences impact everyone. But humanists are natural leaders in the effort because humanists understand that this is the only life we have, and this planet is the only place we have to live it. Unlike many religious organizations and those they support, humanists don't rely on a god to fix things, don't rely on an afterlife to improve our lot, and don't have archaic prohibitions about contraception, abortion, or other means of providing families planning options. That's why population dynamics matter so much to humanists—only humans have the ability to protect our planet.

Perhaps today's greatest challenge is grappling with how to raise worldwide standards of living in an equitable manner while simultaneously addressing the continuously deteriorating environment, upon which our very existence depends. As with other serious questions in humanism, we have to learn from history when we address the present.

2016 AHA Humanist of the Year Jared Diamond's books *Collapse* and *Guns, Germs, and Steel* detail some success stories that worked from bottom up as well as top down. In past Japanese and New Guinean societies, people learned to avoid the devastating environmental effects of deforestation by replanting trees at rates that exceeded harvesting of their natural resources. In the Dominican Republic, much of the same was accomplished with a top down approach that contributed to a radically different reality for the Dominicans as opposed to their Haitian neighbors. While there are declines evident around the world in places where deforestation has gone unchecked, we can gain encouragement from the successes and be optimistic that if we make the effort, such social transformation can and will happen.

I don't have all the answers, but am convinced that we need to act quickly on broad scope measures that will address the strains of overpopulation on our planet and reverse our negative global trajectory. Behavior changes are needed that reduce our ecological footprint. And global lifestyle changes are needed so that we lessen the burden we place on our planet and can live better lives.

While there's no silver bullet answer to the ecological conundrums we now face, waiting for disaster is just not a humanist option, so let's use all we know to alleviate the problems now, and use humanist reasoning to find better solutions for the future.

Church-State Separation

Perhaps the issues that humanists focus on the most are those related to keeping religion and government separate. This is partially a matter of striving to do what's right and partially a matter of self-defense in a society dominated by religion. This often plays out in the public schools. The intrusion of religion into public schools is seen in textbooks that fail to teach what we know about history and science because they don't fit within the narrative of the dominant faith. It's seen in efforts to engage in school-sponsored prayer. It's seen in the use of religious teachers in public schools and religious facilities for public school functions. It's seen in efforts to promote abstinence-only vs comprehensive sex education, which has been shown to increase rates of teen pregnancies. And it's seen when teachers refuse to teach evolution, either because they see it as undermining their beliefs, or because they want to avoid controversy.

Most damaging of all, we see people turning to voucher systems as a solution to problems just magnified by their introduction. The first critical shortcoming of voucher programs is that they divert scarce public funds to help a small group of students at the expense of other students, who must then try to continue in schools that now have even less money with which to try and provide a quality education. The second central drawback of vouchers is that they often are used to fund religious education, and that situation results in taxpayer dollars being inappropriately filtered into indoctrinating kids into one brand of religion. It's just wrong to make atheists and others pay for religious education that tends to condemn them. On top of that, such religious schools aren't subject to the same regulations that public schools face, which is why some fall far below public schools in terms of safety and performance.

Whether in voucher programs, or inserted into public school curriculums and textbooks, or as part of the Pledge of Allegiance kids are asked to say every day, the failure to teach the best of modern knowledge for religious reasons poses a serious threat to our nation's educational system and to current and future students. When schoolchildren are taught religious dogma instead of a credible academic program, their ability to function in the real world and compete for jobs is drastically diminished. Religious teachings should not come at the expense of things like science education, mathematics, literature, and history, which should always be taught based on our best current understanding of them.

Keeping schools secular and neutral doesn't infringe on religious liberty, as author Michelle Goldberg explains in *The Huffington Post*: "The relevant argument, then, is not about whether there will be prayer in public schools. It's about whether there will be government-mandated prayer in public schools. The argument is not whether religion can do good things in people's lives. It's whether the government should fund religion. The argument is not even whether religious groups should contract with the government to provide social services …. It's whether religious groups that do receive taxpayer funds should be permitted to proselytize on the public dime, and to refuse to hire those of the wrong faith."

Parents can ensure that their child gets all the religious instruction they want by attending services at their house of worship, partaking in weekend religious education programs, or through participation in religious youth outreach groups. But parents should know that school time is for learning about the world, and not merely yet another time to talk about religion.

Schools aren't the only battleground in the struggle to keep religion and government apart. We see God imprinted on our money, and God oaths are frequently the default for oaths of public office, armed forces enlistment, citizenship, and more. We see prayers at public meetings. Governmental faith-based initiatives intrude on areas of public activity from housing to prisons to addiction recovery. And sometimes belittled as symbolic issues, the use of religious emblems on public property are also real concerns.

Monuments constructed to serve as memorials for veterans and casualties of wars are serious matters deserving of attention. As long as, public cross memorials stand unaltered, they continue to exclude those soldiers of other faiths, or no faith, who served our nation. Disrespecting our patriotic service members like this is indecent, and it's time for it to change. After all, nobody really believes that Christian Right legal teams are sincere in their statement that the cross is secular, as they claim in our case against the Bladensburg, Maryland, forty-foot cross in the middle of a public road—*American Humanist Association et al v. Maryland-National Capital Park and Planning Commission*. It's time the courts and the general public stop taking these obviously false claims that crosses are nonreligious as honest.

Unfortunately, the Religious Right and its allies in government don't really want to honor all those that served or respect everyone in their communities. Efforts to insert Christian language and symbolism are plainly exclusionary, and fail to honor Jewish, Muslim, Hindu, Buddhist, Sikh, and nonreligious community members. And because of the government's involvement in the sectarian message that they convey, such efforts also violate the spirit of the Establishment Clause of the Constitution which forbids government endorsement of religion.

When we as a country refuse to acknowledge that our diversity is one of our greatest strengths, we dishonor the tens of thousands who fought and died to create a nation where religious views didn't divide us and we were able to unite in our desire to work hard and sacrifice for others and for our country.

One church-state separation issue frequently overlooked is the concept of voting in churches. It's only intuitive that where you vote, and what's visible in the polling location, impacts how you vote. Psychologically, this phenomenon is known as *priming*, where what you are initially exposed to goes on to impact your responses or decisions afterward. That's why there is a political line seventy-five to one hundred feet or more from the polling place over which ads for various campaigns and parties must not cross. It would be an unfair advantage, even intimidating to some, for campaigns to advertise any closer. It's no different with religious messages, many of which have real political consequences.

A Baylor University study published in the *International Journal for the Psychology of Religion* found that having a church in clear sight can influence people's answers to questions. Co-author Wade Rowatt pointed out that the "important finding here is that people near a religious building reported slightly but significantly more conservative social and political attitudes than similar people near a government building." The Baylor study confirms an earlier Stanford University study that shows the same effect when looking specifically at how people's voting place influences their vote. Stanford researcher Jonah Berger said: "Voting in a church could activate norms of following church doctrine. Such effects may even occur outside an individual's awareness." It's high time to stop voting in churches used in some 30 percent of polling places today. They are hardly neutral grounds for the issues of the day and there's no reason to funnel taxpayer dollars to churches via the rental money they receive for the use of their space.

A number of issues not traditionally considered church-state separation issues can also be viewed through the lens of keeping religious entanglement out of government. Since the only real reasons to deny equal rights to LGBTQ Americans surround religion-based prejudice, this too can be viewed as a church-state separation issue. Religious views also inappropriately influence a whole host of other issues from right-to-abortion to access to child care options to securing the right to a death with dignity.

Promoting Peace

Watching the chaos in one country after another in the Middle East, it's easy to feel as though the Arab Winter will never end and that the violence will just spiral upward worldwide. But that's not a foregone conclusion. Steven Pinker states in an article for *Slate*,

"The kinds of violence to which most people are vulnerable—homicide, rape, battering, child abuse—have been in steady decline in most of the world... Wars between states—by far the most destructive of all conflicts—are all but obsolete."

But how can this rosy outlook on violence be possible in the era of the Islamic State of Iraq and the Levant (ISIL), nontheist bloggers being hacked to death, and death sentences for atheists accused of blasphemy? As Ayaan Hirsi Ali pointed out on the *Daily Show*, the spike in violence we see in the Islamic world is part of an emerging reformation where activists are "risking their lives trying to get this change done." Some studies, like one by the World Bank on ethnic violence and economic growth, provide evidence that as societies become more economically developed and stable, instances of violence among different ethnic and religious groups decrease. Another barrier to bloodshed is empathy. Empathy prevents violence because people are less likely to hurt others when they come to understand that we are similar in so many ways. The onset of globalization brought increased opportunities for travel, communication and education about others in many different circumstances, and with it increased empathy.

The growth of peaceful conflict resolution is something that people of all backgrounds, religious or not, have to encourage if we wish to stop religious and ideological extremists from instigating violent reprisals both individually and through governments.

Peaceful resolutions to conflicts, at personal and national levels, are not unattainable aims. Rather, they are rational means of behavior that have time and again resolved problems and prevented dangerous escalations. And such methods are rooted in self-preservation because without them, these dire conflicts can lead to holocausts and global wars. This isn't to say that peaceful solutions to political and personal conflicts are always possible. In rare circumstances, such as full-blown genocides, diplomacy may be insufficient, necessitating the use of force.

By communicating with the opposition and finding common ground, however narrow, human beings have the potential to reduce acts of violence and to promote cooperation on some of the most pressing challenges facing our species. For instance, rather than fighting over freshwater supplies in the near future as global climate change causes drinking water to become a scarce commodity, humanity can work to support research into affordable desalinization technologies by which we can increase our drinking water supplies. We should recognize the practical impact of cooperation and how, in this case, it provides both the direct benefit of new technology and the indirect prevention of wars over scarce resources.

War and violence must be our last resort, and such methods should be seen as no resort at all for the resolution of most disputes. By promoting increased dialog between aggrieved parties and attempting to address their needs with the ultimate goal of a peaceful reconciliation, we can end much of the unnecessary violence that plagues our world and slows our development. We can end the slaughter of one religious group by another and stop the desire for brutal political retribution handed down from one generation to the next in violent war zones. By embracing empathy and overcoming religion and politics' exceptionalist tendencies, we can realize that we are one people living in this one world. Only then can we truly give peace a chance, and thereby give humanity its best chance at survival.

Death with Dignity

While almost all of us agree that life can be a beautiful experience full of wonder, struggle, love, and many worthy experiences, we should also acknowledge that for some it may have become irreversibly painful and unwanted. Some people face this situation in a sustained way and aren't experiencing treatable depression or struggling through a difficult period that can be reversed. Sometimes the trauma associated with disease and the restrictive nature of age transforms continued living into a daily exercise of pain and humiliation with no reason to expect improvement. In such cases, our empathy and compassion dictate that we advocate for a release from such interminable suffering when it is requested.

Since 1959, long before the activism of issue pioneer Jack Kevorkian, and organizations (today led by Compassion and Choices and the Final Exit Network), the American Humanist Association firmly supported the right of those who face incurable suffering to end their lives if they so choose, as long as all possible safeguards against misuse of the law are provided. Like Oregon's Death With Dignity Act, it makes sense to have medical and psychological personnel evaluate people to make sure efforts to alleviate suffering have been attempted, and the individuals are of sound mind when making such an irreversible decision.

This thinking is based in part on the question regarding whether a human being truly "owns" their own life, or if that life belongs to another (i.e., their family, society, or god). Humanists conclude that every single human being has sovereignty over their own body and mind. Therefore, a person has the right to end their own life, and it's up to society to make sure this right is maintained and is not abused by those who might gain from the demise of others.

Consider the story of Anastasia Khoreva, a 105-year-old woman who survived the Russian Revolution and two world wars. Friends said the great-great-great-grandmother had been depressed after being stricken with a lung infection and had expressed a desire to commit suicide. Anastasia ended her life by hanging herself and was discovered by her loved ones shortly after. This case didn't have to end in the tragic way it did. What if, instead of violently killing herself alone in a room and traumatizing those who found her, Anastasia had been allowed a compassionate end-of-life procedure? What if her final moments had been in a bed, surrounded by her loving family and friends as she painlessly drifted into unconsciousness and then died?

Exercising true compassion in situations like this may mean understanding a loved one's desire to break out of the prison of life in which they experience constant torment. We, as outsiders, may feel that prison is more desirable to non-existence, but we must recognize that this choice is not ours. Whether we are family, friends, or politicians, we don't have the right to delay our sense of loss so that people who are in unrelievable pain continue to suffer, nor do we have the right to impose our religious beliefs regarding assisted suicide on others.

Healthcare shouldn't just be focused on prolonging life. It should also work to improve the quality of life of patients and grant them a pain-free escape from suffering after the request is properly evaluated by trained professionals. It's essential to remember that the desire to help another human being is the foundation upon which the modern healthcare system is built. And in that effort, we should realize that occasionally the help desired is a compassionate ending of a life filled with anguish.

As healthcare debates continue, this issue deserves special attention. People like Anastasia Khoreva and her family should not have to suffer the trauma of an undignified and painful death. A solution should be devised to ensure that those who no longer wish to live may go about ending their own lives in a dignified way.

Responsible Scientific Freedom

Humanists hold that the pursuit of knowledge through the scientific method should be as unencumbered as possible. As a society we need such a freedom to gain reasonable certainty. We gain confidence in such knowledge through rigorous standards of theoretical basis (why something works), empirical observation (testability and repeatability of results), and expert peer review (to confirm the theory, methodology, and evidence). Allowing for this to proceed enables all fields of knowledge to advance.

All science should be studied with responsibility. While a number of scientific pursuits may be justified by their technical merits, we must be vigilant against ethical pitfalls, such as engaging in human cloning experimentation when we know the majority of results will be failures and produce offspring with numerous genetic defects. Additional categorical examples of unethical science include human experimentation without informed consent and deliberate infection with disease as well as experimentation that involves resistance to torture.

Research and practices aimed at discovering new information should be tempered by humility, compassion, and caring for all life and our environment. This ensures that what's produced from the scientific process can be best relied upon in assessing the efficacy of our actions and policies to bring about stated principled outcomes in other realms of policy.

Additionally, fields of study shouldn't be limited without cause. Even areas broadly considered to be pseudoscientific in one application may provide interesting avenues for research if studied through the lens of a different discipline. For example, homeopathy may have no pharmaceutical value but may call for study from the perspective of placebo medicine and medical ethics. Research methodology and technical application for all science should incorporate the certainty of the science as well as formal, deliberate, and rigorous ethical standards.

An increasingly common concern is the general public's failure to understand what constitutes sound ethical science, and that's leading to poor decision-making. Perhaps the best example of this is in the area of vaccinations. Based on faith, fear, and faulty information, more Americans are questioning the value of vaccinations and the reasons for being vaccinated. Since religious exemptions to vaccinating children for enrollment in public schools were put into place, plenty of parents, religious or not, have decided not to vaccinate.

According to the National Institutes of Health: "By 2000, immunization had practically wiped out measles in the US. But a measles outbreak in 2005 was traced to one unvaccinated US resident infected during a visit to Europe. The returning traveler infected American children who hadn't been vaccinated because of safety concerns—despite study after study showing that childhood vaccines are safe and effective." The NIH reports that a major health epidemic was thwarted "because enough people in the surrounding communities had already been vaccinated," which allowed health officials to contain and treat the infected individuals. We weren't as lucky with more recent measles outbreaks like the one that was sourced with Amish families in Ohio who failed to vaccinate.

A disease can't spread quickly when a majority of those that come into contact with the contagious are immune. This public resistance effect is called "community immunity," which occurs when most members of a community are protected against a disease, providing little chance for an outbreak. Considering how this process works, the more that are vaccinated, the greater the community immunity effect, and the greater the chance for eliminating a specific disease entirely.

It's worth noting that there are a number of people who will never be immune to certain diseases because vaccines aren't 100 percent perfect, and some people may just be resistant to their benefits. Registered nurse and educator Mary Gallagher, writing for *Global Traveler USA*, tells us that "even those not eligible for certain vaccines—infants, pregnant women and immune-compromised individuals—get some protection because the spread of the disease is contained." This is why it's so critical to vaccinate as many people as possible in order to maximize community immunity and protect those vulnerable few among the vaccinated as well as those who can't vaccinate. Whether they realize it or not, the more parents that choose to opt out of vaccinations, the more likely the diseases we vaccinate for will infect the innocent and possibly even return in force.

Many misinformed parents don't understand why others would complain about their personal opposition to vaccinations, not getting how their decision impacts everyone. They just don't recognize that when whole segments of the population refuse to vaccinate out of fear, all of society becomes more susceptible to deadly diseases. Examples also include those with religiously based moral concerns like the Catholic opposition to cervical cancer vaccination because they think the reduced cancer risk will encourage sex—maybe if they just had to say that aloud they'd realize the ridiculousness of their position.

Humanists acknowledge that science has the capacity to distinguish clearly those claims that are demonstrably false from those that show proven utility to explain the world. By giving researchers the freedom to explore the limits of human knowledge, we'll achieve continual advancement. Such strong understanding and wide acceptance does not mean that all scientific findings are immutable truths. Evolutionary biology, for instance, continues to develop as we build stronger understanding of how it works. However, the expansion of natural selection theory into social Darwinism and eugenics has been discredited as unethical and scientifically illegitimate. This illustration shows how efficacy can be irrelevant when ethics are violated, a concept that applies in other circumstances as well.

Since scientific naturalism is a cornerstone for humanism, emphasis is rightly placed on advocating for scientific integrity. The methods of study and exploration represented by the sciences provide the most reliable tools for understanding the world around us.

CHAPTER 9

Living Humanism

Humanism is an engaged philosophy. We call it a "lifestance" because it doesn't just address a narrow range of thought; it is intended to be a better *way of living* for individuals and for humanity as a whole. It's worth taking a look at life from beginning to end from a humanistic perspective.

Origins

Various religions have their origin myths, which serve a number of functions. They describe where the earth and everything in our environment comes from. They describe in exciting terms how their version of truth came to be revealed. And they offer a shared way of thinking about our environment.

But such tales are increasingly revealed as just myths, for they're completely incompatible with modern understandings of the world. While these tales offer us some cultural insights into the past, they don't afford us much guidance on our journey forward.

Humanism includes no myths whatsoever, origin or otherwise. Instead of imagined tales, we accept the best of modern science's explanations as a starting point for further inquiry. It's a constantly but modestly shifting reference point as we learn more about the universe and adjust our understandings.

For humanists the beginning was about 13.798 billion years ago, when all matter, compacted into a space smaller than a marble, exploded into our expanding universe. Neil deGrasse Tyson said: "Regardless of what you may have read or heard, the Big Bang is supported by a preponderance of evidence and has become the most successful theory ever put forth for the origin and evolution of the universe."

From the first evidence of algae and bacteria that appeared on earth in its first billion years of existence, to the first life on land in the last billion years, to the extremely recent arrival and distribution of humanity throughout the globe over the last few million years, all life as we know it is the result of an evolutionary process where living things are descended from common ancestors. That this fact conflicts with ancient religious tradition is no small matter and helps explain why so many Americans refuse to recognize what we've learned about how we came to be.

Of course, religion itself is evolutionary, beginning likely with animism, the idea that supernatural capabilities reside in everyday objects, from the trees to animals to the sun. As religions evolved to become more complex and hierarchical—and, it should be added, increasingly used by authorities to consolidate and maintain their power—they became so dictatorial and their stories so exaggerated, that it's hardly surprising that some aspects of them seem absurd today. Take, for example, the anthropocentric idea that humans are the most important thing in a universe, even though there are more stars in the sky than there are grains of sand on the earth. This is narrow-minded given today's understanding of the universe, which isn't centered on our planet, our solar system, or our galaxy. But perhaps we can give religious folks a pass on that aspect since grasping a universe as big as ours can stretch the comprehension capabilities of even our most brilliant scientists.

Thinking about our origins and development in this way has philosophical consequences. We understand that we live in a morally neutral world that's part of a vast indifferent universe but have learned that cultivating empathy and compassion can lead people to become more altruistic. We see human influences on our environment and history that, while sometimes negative, are clearly significant in their impacts. Such evidence gives us hope of making changes today that will lead to better outcomes in the future. Combined with evidence of decreasing global violence and examples of continually expanding technological capabilities, we have reason for optimism.

Family

Another beginning to life is seen in our individual births and those of our children. Children may be born into religious families, but they are all born nontheists, having no ingrained beliefs in gods. The consensus I've seen in humanist circles is that it makes sense to let kids learn about religion and decide what to believe or not for themselves. Other than comparing traditional faith and mythology from time to time, railing against religion may have the opposite impact as kids tend to be repelled by negativity.

Other humanist parenting advice I've seen includes resisting the urge to discredit oneself by accepting fables such as "Yes, there truly is a Santa Claus" or inventing convenient stories: "Monsters are afraid of this magic nightlight." It's fine to be creative and participate in dramatic play and storytelling, but when real questions are asked, real answers should be given. Kids may need support when they are confronted with situations where their nontheism is outed, such as in not saying "under God" in the Pledge of Allegiance, but mostly they'll manage on their own.

Indeed, kids may surprise you with their good intuitions on how to handle god questions. When my daughter Johanna, who was five at the time, went with me to visit family on the occasion of her grandmother's death, another little girl asked where we were headed. "Grandma's funeral," Johanna said. "Sorry," said the other girl and added, "She's in heaven now." Johanna simply replied: "We don't believe in heaven, but I'll remember Grandma."

Most good parenting advice is simply good parenting advice and doesn't reference one's beliefs or lack thereof. What we're after is what works in the real world. And in the real world the importance of family, and close friends as well, cannot be overstated. Humanist values are family values.

Sometimes reporters ask me if humanists care about marriage, considering that we don't value a blessing from a clergy person and don't believe in a god who can solemnize a commitment. While I do know some committed humanist couples that haven't chosen marriage, and there are active polyamorous atheist groups, I find those to be the exception rather than the rule. Many humanists value the public commitment to a life partner just as non-humanists do. Humanists don't condemn others for the choices they make regarding consenting adults, but neither are we immune from innate and societally reinforced drives toward couple bonds. This is reinforced by the fact that divorce rates among atheists are among the lowest in America.

Fulfillment

Even if it's not the most profound or lasting in nature, humanists appreciate the temporary fulfillment found in satisfying desire. Humanists take pride in celebrating all that enables us to enjoy life's many pleasures and delights. Viewing human satisfactions physically, mentally, and emotionally, humanists affirm our freedom to live life to the fullest and not be restricted by conventional religious or societal precepts—or any ideology that would arbitrarily limit our choices and self-determination. The humanist philosophy involves fully, yet responsibly, partaking of the various joys life has to offer. The only consideration that need limit us from realizing our nature in a broad variety of contexts is that we be mindful of the wants and needs of others, that we treat them with the respect and dignity all humans deserve.

As discussed in earlier chapters, happiness and well-being are what make life worth living. And as psychologists have confirmed, happiness can be gained through helping others. That's especially true when it comes to doing right by your loved ones, which is just another reason why relationships and family are so central to a good life. It's through relationships that much of our sense of fulfillment is achieved.

In the emphasis we give to family, friendships certainly shouldn't be ignored. Since you choose your friends, not your family, they may be even more central to building your fulfilling life.

Friends share our interests, and we feel mutual empathy for each other that provides a basis for lasting mutual support. Practicing reciprocity in our friendships is a way to connect and build trust so we can rely upon one another in difficult times. Friends can be helpful in small and large ways, and in just being enjoyable to be around. Communities of friends become a social support network that leads to more successful lives.

As we build our empathy for all humanity, we can cultivate a positive sense of awe for what happens around the globe and across history. Humanist long-distance swimmer and writer Diana Nyad captured this in her statement: "I can stand at the beach's edge with the most devout Christian, Jew, Buddhist, go on down the line, and weep with the beauty of this universe and be moved by all of humanity—all the billions of people who have lived before us, who have loved and hurt and suffered."

For many humanists who aspire to make progress on this planet, we also seek to impact the lives of others and the course of events. While achieving accomplishments through work can be beneficial and satisfying, lasting fulfillment isn't gained from feeling safe and comfortable, or from examining a win/loss record. When we look back on what we've accomplished in our work, at home, with family and friends, and through our charity and activism we find meaning in life in the ways we've changed things for the better.

Joy

Today's atheists understand that this life is our sole opportunity for joy, and we'd better make the best of it for ourselves and for the social good. We've come a long way from the days of Madalyn Murray O'Hair. For those who remember her, O'Hair was the quintessential angry atheist. Her days were filled with combating religion, undermining faith, and doing so with a caustic wit.

More common today are the Brad Pitt-Angelina Jolie, or "Brangelina," atheists who spend most of their time trying to help themselves and lift up the world through their good works. Still, even with popular role models like Pitt and Jolie, some people are afraid to part with religious belief. Many Americans, even those who have become disillusioned by their religion, are uncomfortable at the thought of a life without religion. Without a traditional religious framework where would they find meaning or joy? But there's no need to view this freedom with such trepidation. The possibilities for a meaningful and joyful life free from traditional religion are limitless. Knowing how best to solve problems, that you are free from arbitrary constraints of thought, and that you can live a life of real meaning is exhilarating.

In her *Notes from My Travels* Angelina Jolie said: "There doesn't need to be a God for me. There's something in people that's spiritual, that's godlike."

We often hear Christian conservatives like Bill O'Reilly bemoaning that atheists hate Christmas, and it has taken root as a stereotype that assumes atheists are alone and miserable on such holidays. But just because nontheists don't adhere to a particular faith doesn't mean we can't appreciate traditional celebrations. If they like, humanists, atheists, and freethinkers can celebrate Jewish High Holidays, Christian Easter, pagan solstices, and other special days with friends and relatives just like everyone else, without worrying about adhering to the rules of one dogmatic faith. Many humanists I know are such lovers of holidays--so enjoying the opportunities for family, love, and charity—that they also participate in humanist created holidays, like Darwin Day, National Day of Reason, Freethought Day, and Human Light.

Religion isn't just about holiday cheer; it often emphasizes pain over pleasure. Many practice relatively minor acts of asceticism like fasting for Ramadan, forgoing meat during Lent, or dressing in modest clothing. But some go further. A few Catholics in the Philippines volunteer to be non-lethally crucified on Good Friday. Others still engage in self-flagellation. There's also the violent form of jihad practiced by some radical Islamists, the self-mortification of Kabbalah Jews, the purification ceremonies of Native

Americans, and the ritual of circumcision. In these teachings, suffering on earth is considered a badge of honor to be sought out and endured. It's sometimes seen as a prerequisite to an afterlife in heaven. But freed from these unnecessary constraints, humanists are able to live lives where such pain and suffering is viewed as unnecessary, and so understandably avoided. Instead, nontheists can pursue lives rich in satisfaction and gratification.

Of course, religion doesn't just emphasize pain, it sometimes demonizes pleasure too. Religious practices around the world today demonstrate just how negative faith-based approaches to sex can be: genital mutilation, forced marriage, and unpunished rape are just three examples. Here at home, faith-based views of sex hinder the lives of millions of LGBTQ Americans and prevent normal sexual exploration for anyone following the rules too closely. Being free from religion means being free from taboos around contraception, same-sex relationships, oral and anal sex, sex during menstrual cycles, and sex before marriage. There's no need to suffer pangs of guilt for masturbation or consensual sex. Instead humanists are encouraged to enjoy a satisfying, safe, and pleasurable sexual life.

But remember, whether we're enjoying celebrations or seeking sexual pleasures, such freedoms include responsibilities. Figuring out those responsibilities is a good deal less complicated than consulting archaic texts or "received" truths because humanists derive morality from a combination of knowledge, compassion, and the Golden Rule. In order to seek happiness in this framework we need only to avoid harming others. Indeed, we've found that in order to enjoy the highest happiness we need to help others.

Instead of placing emphasis on the supernatural and the afterlife, atheists value the life being lived today. Viewing this life as something to be enjoyed rather than a test one is required to pass before arriving in heaven is conducive to health and happiness. As past AHA president Lloyd Morain explained, people experience life humanistically, be they religious or not, when they enjoy the sights and sounds and other sensations of the world for what they are and are eager for the challenges life puts before us.

A Note on Free Will

Our brains are the only tools we have to make decisions since we, as humanists, believe there is nothing supernatural about our bodies and minds. Following that line of thinking, each of our brains operate from a combination of our individual genetics (nature) along with our accumulated education and experience (nurture). Therefore, some people argue that our alleged "choices" are illusory, for they're a direct result of how our biologies and biographies intertwine. We contemplate options, when time permits, and that contemplation may lead to a different option being executed, but the fact that we contemplated at all, and had time to do so, are beyond our ability to choose. Some thoughtful humanists still debate this, but it certainly appears that free will doesn't actually exist.

In *Free Will* Sam Harris explains that this conclusion, as startling as it is, isn't as problematic as it might seem. Our lives aren't mapped-out in advance; there are countless factors influencing us—and those factors are in constant flux. While you might worry that in a world without free will people will be freed from personal responsibility in a way that may lead to irresponsible behavior, it seems unlikely to go that far since creating the world we want to live in requires acting, to a degree, as if there were free will. Putting in place punishments for crimes isn't a sin upon those who could act in no other way; it's an often important factor in the determination of a potential misdeed. As a society, we need to act as if people have choices in order to place better turns in their path.

Of course, it always makes sense to act thoughtfully and help guide others toward a kinder and more rational path. But it's also sensible to feel compassion for—and act compassionately toward—those who've erred because of some regrettable combination of what they inherited from their family and the environment that they were involuntarily born into.

Death

In a life filled with unknowns, one of the few constants is the certainty of death. Religious people believe that it's normally just the beginning of another life, whether in heaven, hell, or through reincarnation. But for humanists, atheists, and others who reject claims of human existence persisting beyond the brain's functioning, death is the final stage. Nothing, neither good nor bad, comes after that final moment.

While the prospect of permanent non-existence is terrifying for some, it can also be comforting. As humanists, we don't bank on an afterlife unsupported by the evidence. Instead, as John Lennon said, "no hell below us, above us only sky," we live for today. This means that regardless of our spiritual state or acts on earth, there will be no punishment in the beyond. Without an afterlife, we don't blindly follow outdated rules, such as those found in Christian Bibles that prohibit eating pork barbecue, going clean shaven, wearing stretch cotton, or working on Sundays. As the "Great Agnostic" of the nineteenth century, Robert G. Ingersoll, once said: "I would rather live and love where death is king than have eternal life where love is not."

Whether someone is religious or not, dealing with the death of a loved one is never easy. People are understandably vulnerable in such situations. So nobody would be so insensitive as to proselytize at funerals, right? Wrong! How many of us have experienced a priest, minister, or rabbi using a funeral as an excuse to try introducing or reintroducing the grieving into the fold? I've experienced this myself a few times. I objected to the proselytizing in these moments because it excluded and divided people at a time that calls for inclusion and solidarity.

Unfortunately, from the moment an atheist's loved one falls seriously ill, many religious people feel that consoling them with a religious message is appropriate. In reality, statements like "We're praying for them" or "God is watching over them" are no comfort. Such sentiments may alienate the bereaved from family and friends in their time of need. It's even worse to attempt to comfort a dying atheist with god references.

Faced with death, believers seem to think that atheists must recant, but Christopher Hitchens showed us that this is not the case. After being repeatedly confronted with his impending demise from esophageal cancer and the potential benefits of faith, he said with his usual clarity: "No evidence or argument has yet been presented which would change my mind."

Proselytization is even worse when religious family members hold a religious funeral for someone who was clearly not religious while they were alive. When a close atheist friend of mine, Sharon Raine, died unexpectedly in her early twenties, her funeral was among the most drenched in Christianity that I've ever experienced, featuring speeches about her experiencing heaven. To me and other secular friends in attendance, it was clear that trying to "remember" nonbelievers as people of faith is more than just exclusionary—it's disrespectful. It's upsetting when the faithful imbue religiosity into the lives of dead secularists.

This is not to say that atheists want to ban religious family members and friends from talking about their own beliefs at memorial services. For many people, religion is a critical part of navigating the intense grief that comes with the death of a loved one. When religious people want to express their faith to nontheists or others who don't share their faith, the best approach is personalizing their statements. They might say: "For me, it's comforting to believe that they are in a better place." Since their intentions are usually positive, if religious people realize that not everyone resorts to religion to deal with death and that pushing religion upon the deceased or grieving is inconsiderate, then many of these issues will resolve on their own. Broader awareness of secular alternatives is also necessary. The use of Humanist Celebrants, now increasingly popular in the UK, is starting to catch on here in the US. Their services provide a better option for nontheist and interfaith memorials.

As Ingersoll eloquently stated: "We know that through the common wants of life—the needs and duties of each hour—their grief will lessen day by day, until at last this grave will be to them a place of rest and peace—almost of joy. There is for them this consolation. The dead do not suffer. And if they live again, their lives will surely be as good as ours. We have no fear."

Life is a known quantity that should be lived to its fullest by all. Humanists recognize this concept, which is why we try to improve the world we live in instead of preparing ourselves for a life after death. We realize that we will not see our loved ones after we die. And it's precisely because of this that we strive to view every moment of our waking lives as offering us precious opportunities for love and happiness.

Immortality

Some say that inherent in the human psyche is a natural tendency to strive for immortality. From earliest animistic religions and ancestor worship, through the Greek and Roman immortals, through today's notion of heaven, one of the biggest "carrots" of religion is its promise of immortality, and this is also true in the expectation of improving rebirths in Buddhism. Like many religions, Christianity itself is born in the efforts of Jesus to somehow overcome death through resurrection of the body.

Even outside the bounds of religion, people strive for immortality through science, as we see with our ever greater efforts to medically defeat the results of aging on our bodies. While not as popular as it once was, people still try to engage in cryogenics, more recently using vitrification to avoid the creation of ice crystals in order to preserve the mind and body until some future date when the technology may exist to give them a new life. Similarly, ideas still more fit for science fiction than actual science involve long-term hibernation for those that may wish for a future cure to a problem they face today.

While the plane of death still represents a barrier into the unknown, we're constantly learning more about it. We understand that near-death experiences when the heart stops and people have various sensations of light, hovering, and so forth, are natural responses to the brain's failure to receive oxygen. We understand that for something to survive the death of the body and brain living on in an afterlife or rebirth, the mechanics of the transfer process would violate just about everything we know about science. We have every reason to believe that the end of life is an end to our existence in a way difficult for our minds to comprehend. We need not fear death, for as Epicurus explains, we won't be what makes us who we are after we're dead anyway.

But the only true form of immortality is that which we experience from the impact we make while we're still alive. And, over time, like ripples in the water, that impact can extend outwards. We may bring new life, guide the lives of others, and set events in motion. Through activism and support of causes that represent our viewpoints we empower ourselves to influence the course of events.

CHAPTER 10

Becoming an Activist

When we think of being an activist, the first thing that comes to mind is politics. Practically speaking, just as past changes didn't come about in a vacuum, neither will future ones. Humanists, even with their limited acceptance in society, influenced core issues over the past century in many ways. And with our rising numbers and organizational refinements, we can do much more over the present century if we have the courage to act on our convictions.

Political Activism

"Clearly America has deep secular roots, a large population of talented secular individuals, and great appreciation for secularity. It would be a shame to waste this valuable resource by conceding the job of policy making to anti-intellectual religious activists."

–David Niose, *Nonbeliever Nation: The Rise of Secular Americans*

One of the first steps of being an effective political activist is staying informed. Whether it's reading the weekly e-news from TheHumanist.com (sign-up for this now if you haven't already), listening to *Democracy Now*, watching *The Young Turks*, or imbibing traditional and blog media, it's worth keeping abreast of the latest developments in the issues that matter to you.

The next step is taking action on those issues that, personally, you care most about.

When it comes to influencing Congress, the best way to influence officials is in a personal visit. Whether you get to see your

Senator or Representative or their staff, that personal visit has the greatest chance because you can engage in a two-way conversation that may sway their thinking. Visits can be done in-district when the candidate is home or on Capitol Hill in their offices there. Or, if you can attend campaign or other events where you may need to financially contribute to attend, you may discover even greater access and interest in your opinions. You might also support the Freethought Equality Fund political action committee to bring more freethinkers into government working on behalf our shared priorities.

While there are limitless examples of the effectiveness of a personal visit, one that connects to humanism began as the AHA's development director, Maggie Ardiente, filled in on the lobbying front as we were approaching Darwin Day in 2012. Darwin Day, an international celebration of Charles Darwin's birthday founded by Dr. Robert Stephens, is celebrated on February 12 to raise awareness of Darwin's contributions to humanity and the importance of evolution in science classes during a time of a growing 'intelligent design' movement. It became a project of the American Humanist Association just a couple years prior, during which the focus was on encouraging Darwin Day celebrations throughout the AHA's network of local chapters.

I had the idea of reaching out to Rep. Pete Stark (D-CA), the AHA's 2008 Humanist of the Year and the only open humanist serving in Congress, to see if he would be willing to introduce a House Resolution recognizing February 12 as Darwin Day. I thought it might be a long shot, but Maggie was willing to try. She called Jeff Hild, who served as Rep. Stark's legislative director at the time, and arranged to meet with him in person. Prepared with a draft resolution, Maggie talked to Jeff one-on-one about the importance of Darwin Day and asked for Rep. Stark's support in issuing a formal resolution to recognize February 12 as Darwin Day. Not only did Hild and Rep. Stark agree to introduce the resolution, they helped draft additional, stronger language in support of evolution, even adding an item about climate change which, at the time, was being vigorously debated in Congress.

Rep. Stark introduced House Resolution 81 on the floor of the US House of Representatives on February 9, 2011, with the following statement:

> Charles Darwin is worthy of recognition and honor. His birthday should be a time for us to celebrate the advancement of human knowledge and the achievements of reason and science. It should also be a time for Congress and other elected officials to ensure that children are being taught scientific facts and not religious dogma in our public schools. It is also an opportunity to push back against those that seek to undermine the science of climate change for political ends.

We later learned that Rep. Stark was pleased with the positive press received and that hundreds of constituents wrote emails and commented on his Facebook page to show their support. And I was pleased to co-author an article, published via *The Huffington Post*, with Rep. Stark to bring Darwin Day to the general public's awareness.

In addition to lobbying your federal representatives, don't forget to also lobby at the state level. Frequently, it's relatively easy to access state legislators when you can demonstrate your interest and involvement. Many of them are just thrilled to hear that you're interested in their work.

If a visit like the one that began the now annual push for Darwin Day legislation is not an option, due to the timing or other restrictions, the next best way to provide influence is through a phone call where you can still spend time explaining your position and get a response from staff. Phone calls are great even on the day of the vote. Positions stated on the calls are tallied so that politicians have a sense of where their constituents stand.

The first bill I ever lobbied against was the Federal Marriage Amendment, which would have amended the US Constitution to prevent same-sex marriage, undoing the work of the many state courts that ruled bans of same-sex marriage unconstitutional. During this campaign I made many calls to congressional offices and found that engaging in conversations with legislative assistants enabled me to remind liberal representatives to stand up for what's right and remind conservative representatives to allow such decisions to be made at the state level. Working in such a way, the Federal Marriage Amendment was defeated every time it was introduced.

If calls aren't an available option, and you have the time, the next best method is a personal and fully individual snail-mailed letter. These have a slight edge on emails for influencing because they prompt the offices receiving them to send you a response, sometimes crafted just for you, and that gets them thinking about your point of view. But keep in mind that snail mail takes a long time, not just because of the postal mail process, but because letters to members of Congress go through security protocols that increase the delay.

That's one reason why emails can be so effective. Now that congressional offices have developed systems for receiving and tallying emails, their speed and clear usage make them quite useful. You can send them individualized e-mails via their preferred web-form or e-mail address, or customize e-messages to them via organization's systems—such as when you respond to email action alerts from the AHA. They arrive quickly and get tallied quickly.

Social media approaches to members of Congress and their staffs via their official Facebook and other pages provide a growing source of connection. With some principals handling their own Twitter pages, carefully constructed tweets to them may have more impact than traditional means.

While not useless, direct mail postcards that get returned to the organization instead of going directly to the official are likely the least effective means since they take a long time to reach you via direct mail, be returned and processed, and then delivered to their intended recipient's offices in a bulk type format that won't normally be responded to individually. However, seen in bulk, sometimes those responses make a nice media statement.

Occasionally overlooked, an important way to influence both politicians and the general public on political and other issues is through effective use of opinion letters and editorials. Opinion letters sent to traditional print publications, like newspapers and magazines, get read more than nearly every other section in those respective publications. Your opinions in online blog and social media forums also have the potential to influence.

Issue advocacy alone isn't the only way to exercise influence. Don't forget to examine the candidates and ballot initiatives for yourself and vote on Election Day in both the primaries and general elections. With just 36.4 percent voting in the 2014 elections, the lowest since World War II, your vote counts all the more. And you can help others do the same by participating in voter registration drives and helping volunteer at election headquarters to keep elections fair and speedy enough to ensure that everyone gets a chance to vote. You can help prevent hours-long disenfranchising voter lines by helping run them, and while you're there you can make sure the process is kept honest, not excluding valid voters or discouraging them from exercising their rights. And if you see religious proselytizing, you can let the AHA's legal department know so they can fix it.

Just as you can get involved in ensuring fair campaigns, you can also get involved in a specific humanistic candidate's campaign so that they have a better chance of winning. The Freethought Equality Fund mobilizes volunteers for candidates that support humanist issues across the country, and you may also know of locals who specifically could use your help.

Certainly, political activism is a worthwhile endeavor, but it's not the only kind of social activism. Don't forget "checkbook activism." Whether it's supporting the AHA, or our lobbying arm the Center for Freethought Activism, or its election intervention arm the Freethought Equality Fund PAC, or another of the many groups you support, checkbook activism is undeniably one of the most important ways you can make a difference in political and social concerns.

Charitable Activism

While church-goers are well-known as sources for charitable giving, there is a false stereotype that atheists and agnostics are not so generous. The truth is that nontheists, particularly humanists, are extraordinarily generous and active in the entire spectrum of charitable activity. In order to demonstrate this activism, a number of humanist and atheist groups have established charitable programs.

One aspect people tend to overlook when thinking about how much churches do for charity is how much they don't do for charity. According to a *Free Inquiry* article, which mentioned a study reported on in the *Washington Post*, America gives religions over $80 billion a year in charitable funds. But how much of that goes to public good versus lining the pockets of the clergy? While it's difficult to find good data, even an evangelical research project found that 82 percent of average church income is spent on administration, building, and personnel.

For a number of years the American Humanist Association utilized a Humanist Charities project that raised hundreds of thousands of dollars for national and international relief efforts. Among the highlights of this work was that done for the 2010 earthquake in Haiti. Due to humanist charitable work already on the ground and an efficient system for getting funds and resources to the right people, Humanist Charities and AHA-stamped foods and medicine were the first to arrive in the city of Jacmel, helping thousands of people.

In recent years it became clear that the resources necessary to manage a well-operated charity effort, even for relief aid, required specialized staff and consistent attention. It also made sense to do our best to consolidate the movement's charitable endeavors so when we did participate in charitable activism we had the biggest bang for our buck. That's why the AHA merged Humanist Charities into Foundation Beyond Belief (FBB), which is by far the most substantial group in the freethought movement with a focus on humanist generosity and compassion with charitable impact. Humanist Charities became FBB's Humanist Crisis Response program, which is now a focal point for the humanist response to major humanitarian crises. The AHA uses its considerable resources to spread the word and support the charitable activities of FBB and its Humanist Crisis Response program.

Individual activism can start with supporting Foundation Beyond Belief so we humanists can get credit for our good works and dispel the myths about uncharitable atheists and agnostics. But it need not end there. Finding reliable charities is assisted by examining charitable organizations' records on nonprofit rating sites like Charity Navigator and GuideStar, as well as seeing how many of the twenty standards of the Better Business Bureau Wise Giving Alliance the charity meets. When giving and participating personally in local charities one may not be able to use such guides, but by being personally involved and perhaps participating on leadership boards yourself, you can see that your efforts and support are well placed.

Humanists can do much more than supporting disaster relief efforts—we can be active supporting the arts, medical charities, international aid groups, and more. Giving to national advocacy efforts, from the ACLU to Americans United for Separation of Church and State and the American Humanist Association itself, should be particularly prioritized. Humanists understand more than most that direct charitable aid may alleviate problems, but political advocacy has the potential to actually solve them.

Humanism provides what we think is the best way to solve problems, so it makes sense to apply that kind of thinking within charitable endeavors.

The Example of Addiction Recovery

A key illustration of how humanists can have a positive impact by applying humanist values to social challenges is in the area of addiction recovery. Men and women of all ethnic backgrounds and religious or nonreligious affiliations suffer from debilitating addictions which have detrimental effects on millions of lives. Addiction recovery treatments shouldn't discriminate either, but Alcoholics Anonymous (AA) does. AA has demonstrated its willingness to remove affiliated groups that fail to hold to its religious standards, which include a belief in God, as stated in the organization's "Twelve Steps" to recovery.

For AA members, the Twelve Steps dictate a lifestyle code, a strict roadmap away from addiction. If you want to recover from addiction through AA, it's imperative to treat the program as a "higher power," says *The Fix*, a magazine focused on recovery issues. Members are encouraged to recite the Lord's Prayer during meetings, to follow the steps meticulously and without deviance, and to abstain completely from their abused substance. AA insists that recovery be a lifelong process, maintaining that even an addict who has been clean or sober for ten years should continue to come to meetings.

So when secular Toronto-area AA meeting groups Beyond Belief and We Agnostics were unceremoniously kicked out of the organization by the regional chapter association, there was no question that straying from the original God-centric tenets of the Twelve Steps was the driving factor. Both groups had adapted the Twelve Steps to their worldview, which didn't require a supreme being. Instead, they removed all references to God, and utilized a more humanist-centric method of group recovery. AA retaliated by removing them from directories, their website, and existence under the AA umbrella.

Humanists and other atheists and agnostics suffering from addiction now have more modern alternatives. Rather than join a group that actively blocks from membership those without a belief in God, nontheists can seek out other programs that not only accept them, but empower them to overcome addiction by helping develop tools and encouraging mutual support among members. SMART Recovery (Self Management And Recovery Training) is one program pioneering an individualistic, non-proselytizing approach for people of any, or no, religious background.

Joseph Gerstein, the SMART Recovery founding president, describes the program as "science-based, incorporating validated approaches," as opposed to the Twelve Step program used by AA, which makes the individual dependent on God, faith, and the meetings themselves. AA, he says, is "abstinence-focused," whereas SMART Recovery meetings aim to help people whose goal isn't necessarily to abstain from drinking altogether. He also notes that several legal cases in the United States have unanimously ruled that Alcoholics Anonymous is "pervasively religious," and, as of 2007, judges and parole offices can no longer order that particular program as once was frequently done.

What truly makes SMART Recovery stand apart from AA's Twelve Step program is its 4-Point Program. Aside from the cosmetic difference of having a third of the guiding tenets, any mention of God is conspicuously absent. The 4-Point Program emphasizes that recovery is in the hands of the person with the addiction. Only he or she can follow through on recovery, by self-motivating, restricting urges, problem-solving, and adapting to a sober lifestyle. Gerstein stresses that the program works to empower the individual, and most importantly, assist him or her in moving beyond the addiction, and eventually move on from the program. It doesn't seek to ensnare anyone for life, which might only remind someone of past addiction and continue—negatively and unnecessarily—to label them as alcoholic.

SMART Recovery isn't designed for nontheists alone. Gerstein estimates that approximately one-third of participants are atheists, agnostics, or humanists of some sort. Another third are "passively religious," or spiritual in some sense. The final third he says are actively religious. The diversity in membership speaks to the success of its humanistically derived approach. Rather than a strict path toward recovery, SMART emphasizes an approach tailored toward each individual's needs, based on scientifically proven methods and cognitive behavioral psychology. A prescription-drug addicted parent of three in Wichita, Kansas, would not pursue sobriety the same way as a crack-cocaine addicted prisoner in California, or an anorexic teenager in upstate New York.

Programs like SMART Recovery provide an alternative for those looking for self-empowerment, unbiased support, and a scientific approach to overcoming their addiction.

Community Activism

Acting locally means getting involved in one's home town in a meaningful way. It may seem like face-to-face encounters are tough places to change minds, but it's those methods that are the most effective. We just can't set overly high expectations. Keep in mind that the average Mormon missionary only converts 3.5 people per year. Considering we're not going door-to-door telling folks there are no gods, we should recognize that it's a slow process to change minds in a humanist direction. But that doesn't mean we can't open up minds to skeptical thinking and help folks see benefits in a society aiming for progress.

If you're interested in getting involved, check out the listing of local groups on the American Humanist Association's website. There may be a humanist group active in your town already that you can join and take part in. If nothing is found there, you might also try SecularDirectory.org which lists an expanding number of atheist, ethical, freethought groups, likely thousands by the time you read this. If you still find no luck, be sure to search your preferred terms on MeetUp.com and other community listings. And if all that fails, and you're interested in starting your own group, call the AHA's headquarters and we'll help as best we can.

Unlike city-sized Pentecostal churches, most humanist and secular groups are comfortably smaller, with under a hundred regular participants. While growth is great, the small size has some advantages in terms of your ability to get to know everyone and get quickly involved in leadership, if that's your interest. Once connected, you can engage in social activities or seek to expand your thinking by hearing talks on various subjects, or you also might participate in community activism. If it's not happening, encourage the leadership to start it, or become a leader and start it yourself. Community activism can take many forms.

All the political activism discussed above can occur in a community setting, and you can be sure that if you take a handful of your members, representing a whole in-district community group to see a representative, they'll be even more willing to work for you than if you go alone. That's true with your federal representatives as well as your state and local ones. In addition to grassroots lobbying, your group could engage in get-out-the-vote campaigns and even engage in candidate forums if they are strictly unbiased in their planning and implementation. Some folks may be concerned that getting political will shed members who disagree, but remember that it will also attract like-minded folks who want to be part of a group that actually *does* something.

Just as individuals do, the community group can be a charitable activist, giving to good causes and participating in them. Think of the power of persuasion of thirty humanist activists proudly wearing humanist T-shirts engaged in a highway cleanup, or a low-income housing project, or a food drive. It really demonstrates how we can be good without a god.

Part of participating in a group is finding ways to bolster the community and keep it healthy and growing. Sometimes that means checking in with a sick member, spending time getting to know people, or just greeting newcomers in a friendly way.

While humanists tend to enjoy friendly debate and appreciate divergent views for how they can help us learn more about issues, there are some limits required in order to maintain a healthy community. It's a rare occurrence, but I have encountered a few people who wanted to be fully accepted members of a humanist group and have their views validated as humanistic, but who were clearly not humanists. It's not just that they had a few conclusions out of sync with what humanists tend to conclude, but they saw the world in an entirely different light with frequent conservative positions on abortion, LGBTQ rights, environment, and so on. Perhaps such individuals are just having a tough time finding community, but they can create a real challenge for the groups wanting to keep their doors open to all, but not wanting to be thwarted by negativity or prevented from being outspoken advocates on core humanist issues. In such cases where a member's negativity is sapping the group of its vitality, the best course is to part ways and move forward.

Another way to help the local community, actively get the word out about humanism, and act on humanist values is to become a Humanist Celebrant. Endorsed by the AHA's adjunct, the Humanist Society, Humanist Celebrants can perform legal wedding ceremonies in all fifty states and the District of Columbia in addition to several countries. When family and friends of a couple participate in a humanist wedding, it communicates the joy and meaning people can have outside traditional religion. Humanist Celebrants also perform ceremonies for memorial services and other life-cycle events. And we're working to have another way to help communities by endorsing Humanist Chaplains that may someday serve in the military.

HUMANIST CHAPLAINS AND NON-RELIGIOUS AMERICANS IN THE U.S. MILITARY

3.6% of the military identifies as Humanist, and there are more atheists in the military than any non-Christian denomination

23% OF U.S. MILITARY SOLDIERS claim "no religious preference" thus indicating a secular values system

Evangelicals are represented in the Chaplain Corps at over **3 times** the rate of the general population

150 DEMOCRATS in the House supported a bill that would allow Humanist Chaplains in the military

The Netherlands have **38** HUMANIST Chaplains in their military (out of 150 total)

Foxhole Atheists serve in over: 20 COUNTRIES, all 50 STATES, over 100 MILITARY INSTALLATIONS and SHIPS

Why a Humanist Chaplain and Not a Military Psychologist?

- Humanist Chaplains have good answers to "ultimate questions" such as "What happens when you die?" or "How do I find meaning in life?"
- Meeting with a Humanist Chaplain is fully confidential and does not appear on your military record

Sources:
http://militaryatheists.org/network/
DoD & Religion Report: http://militaryatheists.org/demographics/
DoD Demographics Report: http://www.militaryonesource.mil/12038/MOS/Reports/
http://militaryatheists.org/demographics/
-DEOMI Religious Identification and Practices Survey, 2009
-Defense Manpower Data Center, 2012

Infographic created by
AMERICAN HUMANIST ASSOCIATION MAAF
americanhumanist.org

I've never experienced anything so powerful as a humanist celebration of a life recently lost—instead of focusing on scriptures and platitudes, it focuses on the person everyone there cared for deeply, and reminds and informs all present of the person's lasting legacy. Participating in such life occasions are another form of acting on humanist ideals.

Reaching the Next Generation

A special kind of thought process and action is needed if we want humanist advocacy efforts to continue into the future. Traditionally attracting an older, more contemplative crowd, the humanist and atheist movement must broaden itself to reach nontheists of all ages.

In order to do this effectively, it makes sense to look at what works. The success of the originally UK-based Sunday Assembly is demonstrated by the hundreds of young people it has drawn to the non-religious movement, who appear weekly at those gatherings. Sunday Assemblies are not like traditional church services with a preacher at the pulpit and mindless repetition of the same phrases over and over again. Think of them more like entertainment—a karaoke bar or group sing-along, perhaps, with a little intellectual or aesthetic stimulation thrown in. People in their 20s and 30s are particularly attracted to these events that occur in venues like community centers or theaters rather than staid houses of worship. Avoiding awkward religious hymns nobody knows, attendees enjoy popular tunes and classic rock. Speakers are brief, no more than several minutes each, and many conduct poetry readings or showcase artwork rather than reciting from ancient philosophies or texts. And the entire organization is led by young, dynamic entertainers. Sunday Assembly's founders are comedians Sanderson Jones and Pippa Evans, who keep folks entertained with clapping games and more.

Forming groups and events like these, and encouraging our friends and kids to attend them is a way to hook the next generation on humanism. For many young people, they are looking to socialize and have a good time. It's that simple. Late teens and twenty-somethings want to meet new friends. They're often singles actively looking for dates and mates. And since many are recently-minted atheists, they're naturally very critical of religion. They have no negative associations with "atheist," and most never even heard of Madalyn Murray O'Hair. Their atheist heroes are people like Richard Dawkins, Bill Nye, and Gloria Steinem."

If you belong to a humanist community, or are in the process of starting one and want younger people to attend your meetings and be members of your group, you'll need to actively cater to their needs by introducing more fun-driven activities. Once you know what to look for, create the activities that will diversify the ages involved.

While you are at it, if you want your local groups to be as successful as possible, include a variety of activities so there's something for everyone. Not everyone is looking for a once-a-month, lecture-style meeting. The more options there are the better. Tying activities to major holidays and events is a great way to get new people involved, and volunteering is an important component of humanist activism. Hiking groups or other outdoor activities during the warmer months are popular. Humanist Happy Hours or Drinking Skeptically events give opportunities for socializing. Get creative and try group baseball games, karaoke nights, and game nights. Create meetings around programs like the State of the Union, televised debates, science shows like Neil deGrasse Tyson's *Cosmos* series, or even the Academy Awards. Consider activities around activism and the arts. If there is someone in your local group who is passionate about local politics or laws, then have that person lead opportunities to rally at the State Capitol, or initiate a letter-writing campaign to your state officials. Even if not a lot of people show up for the first or second event, keep doing it. Make it consistent. A lot of people hesitate to join the first meeting, but they may well do so eventually.

Now that you know what will draw in folks of all ages, be sure to advertise where people will see it. Older groups used to use just the religion section of the local newspaper. Though that may get some results, get on Facebook and Twitter. Keep these maintained heavily with news, happenings, memes, and popular images as many people aren't even browsing websites anymore. Local groups must be on MeetUp which is where many people in a community look to find like-minded people. All events should be posted there.

Helping new members understand humanism is key. Consider setting up a "What's Humanism?" meeting once a month or every two months and advertise it to the general public. This is a great way to attract new people in a smaller setting, and it's an opportunity for them to ask questions in a comfortable space. Providing free food and drink is another good way to draw them in. You could also make it even more general. Call the meeting "Doubts About Religion?" which will really attract younger people who are likely to not know what humanism is, but definitely question their religious upbringing. Either way, these meetings should be led by only one or two people, and should only include new people.

Need more suggestions? Always make sure that new members are greeted personally before or after the meeting so they feel welcome and also inform them about various events they can attend. Consider finding a volunteer who can lead a child care program during your lecture meetings to bring in younger parents and children. The most successful groups keep at it with these ideas, try them multiple times before moving on, and advertise as much as possible through traditional means and social media. People will come.

More Activism

Political and charitable activities aren't the only ways you can be an activist.

Consumer and shareholder activists look to use their money (beyond donations) in a way that promotes their views. Everyone buys stuff, so everyone is a consumer, and we can carefully monitor what we buy to make sure the companies we support and the products we use are in line with our values. Examples include buying recycled products and ones relatively safe for the environment and buying products that don't needlessly test on animals. Specifically buying from companies like Ben & Jerry's and Annie's Homegrown that have good reputations for practices and donations to humanist causes, and avoiding companies like Hobby Lobby and Chick-Fil-A that aim to impose their conservative religion on the rest of us, is also a form of activism. Shareholder activism takes that up a notch since it entails using one's status as a stockholder in various companies to advocate for those companies to act in socially responsible ways. Coordinated shareholder activist campaigns involve introductions of shareholder resolutions, negotiations with management, and similar techniques.

Art and literature have been used for activism for thousands of years, and often with a mind toward humanistic progress. Art professor Grant Kester argues that, in its many forms, art finds its most legitimate expression when it takes on an activist orientation. Images like the peace symbol and the raised fist convey meaning and offer something to rally around. Paintings, poetry, music, and literature offer a way to subtly critique authoritarian regimes from within, mobilizing and communicating with those who support resistance. Historical examples abound, from the poetry of Francesco Petrarca, who some called the "father of humanism," to the history-making humanist cartoons of Herb Block, to the modern journalists who dare to offer anything that critiques Islam in the face of potential terrorism from Islamists. Philosopher George Santayana made clear that art not only can be a source for secular inspiration but is actually its highest form when he said: "Naturalistic poets abandon fairy land, because they have discovered nature, history, the actual passions of humankind. Their imagination has reached maturity." Just as past movements embraced art to hone their ideas and bring their messages to wider audiences, so should the humanist movement.

While I find humanists aren't particularly likely to be sports fans, it still can be an avenue for indirect humanist activism. Participating as a humanist parent and coach provides countless opportunities for teachable moments for children on the team. People can appreciate sports for many reasons, including recognizing it as another opportunity for us rule-making animals to set boundaries. And we can do this while remembering that it's just a game. It's also a chance to practice our humanistic behavior in friendly competition and use the opportunities for interaction to strengthen our empathy for others.

Whether it be through persuading politicians, using our checkbook, creatively rethinking charitable approaches, getting involved locally, buying with a conscience, finding our message in music, or displaying our humanism in competition, we should explore every opportunity to implement beneficial humanist change in our society.

CHAPTER 11

Conclusions Aren't Enough

Humanism is a positive rational philosophy that aims for personal and societal growth. It means having morals without blind faith, convictions without dogma, and optimism without wishful thinking. It helps us make conclusions about the world we live in and the best ways to behave toward others. But conclusions aren't enough. If we want to create change, we have to get active.

To halt regression and move steadily toward progress, the first task is to acknowledge that it can be done. Humanists hold a rational, pragmatic view of our world and can look to history's numerous examples of committed people making lasting positive changes—from replacing Europe's divine right rulers with elected representatives, to tearing down South Africa's apartheid government, to enabling women to participate in democracy. If we want to make the tide of humanism rise, we must build upon our democratic outlook, our integrity, our historic achievements, and our ability to reach out to some of the greatest thinkers and progressive leaders of our time. We must build upon our connections with religious and nonreligious advocacy groups. We must mobilize our growing numbers online and off. Most importantly, we must recognize that doing all this is just stepping up to the plate. Then we have to play ball.

Humanism could be the philosophic foundation for progressives who otherwise lack any coherent coalescing approach to their views. Humanism can replace the role outdated religion held for many, helping people navigate their personal path to the good. Humanists should be looked to as the trendsetters for a modern rational approach. Credentials in education, compassion, and reason (i.e., credentials in humanism) should be key assets for political, social, and academic success.

The next step is for us to harness our optimism and conviction that change is needed, and use that energy to put our humanist values in action. We need to support humanism with our funding and with our outreach to politicians and our communication with the media.

Personally, we can come out as humanists at every opportunity. Borrowing from humanist Theodor Geisel, also known as Dr. Seuss: "When they reach the sounding off place they shout at the top of their lungs, 'I AM I! ME! I am I! And I may not know why but I know that I like it. Three cheers! I AM I!'" We may face challenges in coming out to our family and friends, and it may even impact our careers in negative ways, but being open and proud has its rewards. More importantly, the more of us who do come out, the faster those negative repercussions will disappear.

When considering which identity to emphasize in our humanist/freethought/nontheist communities, reflect on the fact that you can use more than one, and keep in mind the benefits of humanism. Humanism is a positive identification that speaks about what you do care about, as opposed to only what you don't. I am a non-smoker, a non-physicist, and a non-German speaker, and as much as those aspects may have meaning, they aren't what's important to know about me. In the society we happen to live in, my absence of a belief in a god is a relevant component of my identity, but it doesn't define who I am. Humanism does that better than any other description.

Explaining humanism to others and communicating how it's a viable ethical option for individuals, families, and communities goes a long way toward making this way of thinking more widely embraced. Hearing that friends and family are humanist, finding out that what it means isn't too scary, and realizing the commonalities it has with other forms of progressive thought help people tolerate it, accept it, and maybe even try it for themselves.

When we talk about humanism and humanist issues, it's critical that we frame the debate in our own terms. Cognitive linguist

George Lakoff explains how words and phrases invoke a set of thinking and images in our brains, and how those "frames" significantly influence our opinions of the issue being presented. The Religious Right has a history of framing our issues in terms that disingenuously promote their own points of view. For example, legislation that allows religious military chaplains to discriminate against people based on their religion is called the "Military Religious Freedom Act." Legislation giving religious individuals special exemptions from Obamacare is called the "Equitable Access to Care and Health Act." We don't have to copy their dishonest tactics, but we can appreciate the benefits of framing issues in a way that furthers our cause. Instead of saying, "Let's take God out of the Pledge of Allegiance," we can say, "Let's restore the Pledge to its universal form" and be upfront about why removing "under God" accomplishes that goal. By engaging in smarter activism that rallies people to our side rather than scaring them away, we'll be on our way to occupying a bigger seat at the table.

We can't accomplish these ends by ourselves. We need to seek allies for every effort, within and outside of humanism, often working with religious friends to accomplish mutual aims. When we join forces with the faithful we should remain proud of our humanism and avoid adjusting our standards to accommodate superstitious thinking. Humanists don't need to (and shouldn't) modify what we mean by humanism to have beneficial connections with others. Our convictions are based on knowledge and experience of what is best for ourselves and society and need not rely on faith—belief without evidence. In working with others, we should resist efforts to widen the tent of humanism to include them as part of our identity, because doing so would mean redefining who we are and losing the benefits of our more successful approach to solving problems.

We need to mobilize our allies, and ourselves, and work with those of like mind, to insert humanist positions into the debate about the issues of the day. By this means we can push the course of society in the direction of progress and turn the hopeful optimism of *Humanism and Its Aspirations* into secular prophecy.

Are we going to cause the tide of humanism to rise? If so, we must unite, build on our foundation, connect supportive communities, evolve our strategies, and perhaps most of all, raise public awareness of the positive lifestance of humanism.

Acknowledgements

For their help with research, editing, ideas, and more, I'd like to thank Maggie Ardiente, Janet Asimov, Jennifer Bardi, Bo Bennett, Bob Bhaerman, Matthew Bulger, Carl Coon, Fred Edwords, Luis Granados, Rebecca Hale, Tony Hileman, Jennifer Kalmanson, Mel Lipman, Jan Melchior, Merrill Miller, David Niose, Tony Pinn, Leon Seltzer, Herb Silverman, Lyle Simpson, Mike Werner, Jessica Xiao, and Lisa Zangerl.

I'd also like to recognize the contributions of those who've come before me and also contributed to the thinking that went into this work. Among them are: Clark Adams, Beverly Church, Jane Holmes Dixon, Joe Fox, Christopher Hitchens, Corliss Lamont, Lloyd Morain, Sherwin Wine, and especially Warren Wolf.

Appendices

HUMANISM AND ITS ASPIRATIONS

This third Humanist Manifesto is a successor to the Humanist Manifesto of 1933.

Humanism is a progressive philosophy of life that, without supernaturalism, affirms our ability and responsibility to lead ethical lives of personal fulfillment that aspire to the greater good of humanity.

The lifestance of Humanism—guided by reason, inspired by compassion, and informed by experience—encourages us to live life well and fully. It evolved through the ages and continues to develop through the efforts of thoughtful people who recognize that values and ideals, however carefully wrought, are subject to change as our knowledge and understandings advance.

This document is part of an ongoing effort to manifest in clear and positive terms the conceptual boundaries of Humanism, not what we must believe but a consensus of what we do believe. It is in this sense that we affirm the following:

Knowledge of the world is derived by observation, experimentation, and rational analysis. Humanists find that science is the best method for determining this knowledge as well as for solving problems and developing beneficial technologies. We also recognize the value of new departures in thought, the arts, and inner experience—each subject to analysis by critical intelligence.

Humans are an integral part of nature, the result of unguided evolutionary change. Humanists recognize nature as self-existing. We accept our life as all and enough, distinguishing things as they are from things as we might wish or imagine them to be. We welcome the challenges of the future, and are drawn to and undaunted by the yet to be known. Ethical values are derived from human need and interest as tested by experience. Humanists ground values in human welfare shaped by human circumstances, interests, and concerns and extended to the global ecosystem and beyond. We are committed to treating each person as having inherent worth and dignity, and to making informed choices in a context of freedom consonant with responsibility.

Life's fulfillment emerges from individual participation in the service of humane ideals. We aim for our fullest possible development and animate our lives with a deep sense of purpose, finding wonder and awe in the joys and beauties of human existence, its challenges and tragedies, and even in the inevitability and finality of death. Humanists rely on the rich heritage of human culture and the lifestance of Humanism to provide comfort in times of want and encouragement in times of plenty.

Humans are social by nature and find meaning in relationships. Humanists long for and strive toward a world of mutual care and concern, free of cruelty and its consequences, where differences are resolved cooperatively without resorting to violence. The joining of individuality with interdependence enriches our lives, encourages us to enrich the lives of others, and inspires hope of attaining peace, justice, and opportunity for all.

Working to benefit society maximizes individual happiness. Progressive cultures have worked to free humanity from the brutalities of mere survival and to reduce suffering, improve society, and develop global community. We seek to minimize the inequities of circumstance and ability, and we support a just distribution of nature's resources and the fruits of human effort so that as many as possible can enjoy a good life.

Humanists are concerned for the well-being of all, are committed to diversity, and respect those of differing yet humane views. We work to uphold the equal enjoyment of human rights and civil liberties in an open, secular society and maintain it is a civic duty to participate in the democratic process and a planetary duty to protect nature's integrity, diversity, and beauty in a secure, sustainable manner.

Thus engaged in the flow of life, we aspire to this vision with the informed conviction that humanity has the ability to mold our own fate and to progress toward our highest ideals. The responsibility for our lives and the kind of world in which we live is ours and ours alone.

To view online, please visit: http://americanhumanist.org/Humanism/ Humanist_Manifesto_III

"Humanist Manifesto" is a trademark of the American Humanist Association.

© 2003 American Humanist Association

TEN COMMITMENTS
Guiding Principles for Teaching Values

Altruism

Altruism is the unselfish concern for the welfare of others without expectation of reward, recognition, or return. Opportunities for acts of altruism are everywhere in the family, the classroom, the school, and the wider community. Think of examples of altruistic acts in your experience. What person-to-person and group projects, classroom and community service projects might you and others undertake?

Caring for the World Around Us

Everyone can and ought to play a role in caring for the Earth and its inhabitants. We can directly experience the living things in our homes and neighborhoods like trees, flowers, birds, and insects. Gradually we expand our neighborhood. We learn about deserts and oceans, rivers and forests, the wildlife around us and the wildlife elsewhere. We learn that we are dependent on each other, on the natural world, and all that lives in it for food and shelter, space and beauty.

Critical Thinking

We gain reliable knowledge because we are able to observe, report, experiment, and analyze what goes on around us. We also learn to raise questions that are clear and precise, to gather information, and to reason about the information we receive in a way that tests it for truthfulness, accuracy, and utility. From our earliest years we learn how to think and to share and challenge our ideas and the ideas of others, and consider their consequences. Practice asking "what next?" and "why?" and "how do I/you/we know that?"

Empathy

We human beings are capable of empathy, the ability to understand and enter imaginatively into another living being's feelings, the sad ones and the happy ones as well. Many of the personal relationships we have (in the family, among friends, between diverse individuals, and amid other living things) are made positive through empathy. With discussion and role-playing, we can learn how other people feel when they are sad or hurt or ignored, as well as when they experience great joys. We can use stories, anecdotes, and classroom events to help us nurture sensitivity to how our actions impact others.

Ethical Development

Questions of fairness, cooperation, and sharing are among the first moral issues we encounter in our ethical development as human beings. Ethical education is ongoing implicitly and explicitly in what is called the "hidden curriculum" that we experience through the media, the family, and the community. Ethics can be taught through discussion, role-playing, story telling, and other activities that improve analysis and decision making regarding what's good and bad, right and wrong.

Global Awareness

We live in a world rich in cultural, social, and individual diversity, a world where interdependence is increasing rapidly so that events anywhere are more likely to have consequences everywhere. Much can be done to prepare the next generation for accepting the responsibility of global citizenship. Understanding can be gained regarding the many communities in which we live through history, anthropology, and biology. A linguistic, ethnic, and cultural diversity are present in the classroom and provide lessons of diversity and commonality. We help others reach understanding about the interconnectedness of the welfare of all humanity.

Humility

We must always remember that there's a lot we don't know about the universe. There's still so very much to learn. Science will help us. But sometimes scientists discover surprising things that tell us how some of our old beliefs are false. So we need to be willing to change when our knowledge changes. A good humanist doesn't try to be sure of things that science can't show are true.

Peace and Social Justice

A curriculum that values and fosters peace education would promote the human rights of all people and understanding among all nations, cultural and religious groups. Students should have opportunities to learn about the United Nations' role in preventing conflict as well as efforts to achieve social justice in the United States. They should learn about problems of injustice including what can be done to prevent and respond to these problems with meaningful actions that promote peace and social justice and that protect the inherent human rights of everyone both at home and abroad.

Responsibility

Our behavior is morally responsible when we tell the truth, help someone in trouble, and live up to promises we've made. Our behavior is legally responsible when we obey a just law and meet the requirements of membership or citizenship. But we also have a larger responsibility to be a caring member of our family, our community, and our world. Stories and role-playing can help students understand responsibility and its absence or failure. We learn from answering such questions as: What happens when we live in accordance with fair and just rules? What happens when we don't? What happens when the rules are unjust?

Service and Participation

Life's fulfillment can emerge from an individual's participation in the service of humane ideals. School-based service-learning combines community service objectives and learning objectives with the intent that the activities change both the recipient and the provider. It provides students with the ability to identify important issues in real-life situations. Through these efforts we learn that each of us can help meet the needs of others and of ourselves. Through our lifetime, we learn over and over again of our mutual dependence.

© 2012 Humanist Education Center of the American Humanist Association

GLOSSARY OF MOVEMENT TERMINOLOGY

Atheist – Someone who doesn't have a belief system that includes a god or gods.

Agnostic – Someone who's not sure whether or not there is a god or gods and doesn't see a clear path to finding out.

Antitheist – A person whose convictions lead them to work against theism.

Antireligious – A person who challenges religious institutions and structures regardless of what they believe.

Bright – A person with a naturalistic worldview that has a commitment to civic responsibility.

Community of Reason – A term for the movement of nontheists.

Conservative – Someone who wants to maintain the way things are or go back to the way they used to be, usually in a social context, though there are fiscal conservatives as well.

Dogma – A set of beliefs, most typically concerning the supernatural, the truth of which is assumed to be absolute and unchangeable.

Godless – A person without belief in gods.

Empathy – The identifying with and feeling for another person or group and their situation.

Faith – Trusting or believing in something without evidence.

Freethinker – Someone who refuses to conform and is skeptical about conventional wisdom, especially that involving traditional religion.

Heathen – Someone without membership in a mainstream religion.

Heretic – Someone who dissents from accepted dogma, without necessarily being nontheist.

Humanist – A person who adheres to a progressive philosophy of life that, without supernaturalism, affirms the ability and responsibility to lead ethical lives of personal fulfillment that aspire to the greater good of humanity.

Ignostic – A person who believes the concept of god is incoherent.

Infidel – Someone who is unfaithful to the prevailing religion or religions.

Liberal – Today, this refers to someone who stresses liberty and equality and the political ideas that derive from those stances.

Lifestance – Like worldview, an umbrella category including both religions and philosophies.

Naturalist – One who believes only in the physically observable universe, and not in any supernatural power beyond it.

Nonbeliever – A person characterized by not believing in a religion or faith.

None – A person who doesn't adhere to any particular religious denomination, but may still believe in certain religious precepts.

Nontheist – Someone who doesn't believe in gods, but wants to distinguish themselves from anti-theists.

Pantheist – A person who sees nature and the universe as divine.

Progressive – Someone who is politically or socially committed to government policies of change to achieve the advancement of society.

Rationalist – A person who determines knowledge by emphasizing reason and logic, as opposed to dogma.

Religious – A person who accepts the traditional communal and ceremonial structure of organized religion, but may or may not accept its beliefs in the supernatural.

Secular – Either a person who isn't religious, or anything that's not religious.

Skeptic – Anyone who tends to doubt things until presented with convincing evidence.

Theist – A person whose belief system includes at least one god.

BIBLIOGRAPHY

Alesina, Alberto, and Eliana La Ferrara. "A Test of Racial Bias in Capital Sentencing." *The American Economic Review* 104 (2011): 3397-3433.

Asimov, Isaac (1989) Isaac *Asimov Speaks*. The Humanist. September/October 1989, p 30.

Asimov, Janet (2006) *Notes For a Memoir: On Isaac Asimov, Life And Writing*. Prometheus Books.

Associated Press. "Military probes atheist GI's harassment claims." NBC News, September 22, 2007.

Associated Press. "Woman says trooper asked about faith during stop." *Channel 8 TV*, October 6, 2014.

Bakalar, Nicholas. "On Evolution, Biology Teachers Stray From Lesson Plan." *New York Times*, February 7, 2011.

"New Marriage and Divorce Statistics Released," Barna Group, accessed January 10, 2009.

"Why do some Catholics self-flagellate?" *BBC News*, November 24, 2009.

Bennett, Bo. *Positive Humanism: A Primer*. Sudbury, MA: eBookIt, 2014.

Bernstein, Lenny. "Authorities still trying to determine how measles outbreak began at Disney parks." *Washington Post*, February 17, 2015.

Bohlken, Anjali Thomas; Ernest John Sergneti (2010) *Economic growth and ethnic violence*. Journal of Peace Research. 47(5) 589-600.

Bonner, Michael. *Jihad in Islamic History: Doctrines and Practice*. Princeton, NJ: Princeton University Press, 2006.

Cain, Fraser. "Are There More Grains of Sand Than Stars?" *Universe Today*, November 25, 2013.

Capehart, Jonathan. "From Harvey Milk to 58 Percent." *Washington Post*, March 18, 2013.

Cave, Stephen. *Immortality*. New York: Crown Publishing, 2012.

Corriveau, Kathleen H., Eva E. Chen, and Paul L. Harris. "Judgments About Fact and Fiction by Children From Religious and Nonreligious Backgrounds." *Cognitive Science*, July 3, 2014.

Carlin, George. *Brain Droppings*. New York: Hyperion Books, 1997.

Cohn-Sherbok, Dan. *Atlas of Jewish History*. New York: Routledge, 1994.

Colcord, Willard Allen. "American state papers bearing on Sunday legislation." *The Religious Liberty Association*, 1890.

Cooper, Rob. "Christians Nailed to crosses in gruesome Good Friday re-enactment of Jesus's death in the Philippines." *Daily Mail*, April 6, 2012.

Cote, Richard. *Strength and Honor: The Life of Dolley Madison*. Mount Pleasant, SC: Corinthian Books, 2004.

Cowell, Jason M., Jean Decety, Kang Lee, Randa Mahasneh, Susan Malcolm-Smith, Bilge Selcuk, and Xinyue Zhou. "The Negative Association between Religiousness and Children's Altruism across the World." *Current Biology*, November 5, 2015. www.cell.com/current-biology/abstract/S0960-9822(15)01167-7

Americans United for Separation of Church and State. "FDR D-Day Prayer To Be Added To DC World War II Memorial." *Church and State*, 2014.

Cowell, Jason M., Jean Decety, Kang Lee, Randa Mahasneh, Susan Malcolm-Smith, Bilge Selcuk, and Xinyue Zhou. The Negative Association between Religiousness and Children's Altruism across the World. *Current Biology*, November 5, 2015. www.cell.com/current-biology/abstract/S0960-9822(15)01167-7

Dawkins, Richard. *The God Delusion*. New York: Bantam Books, 2006.

DelReal, Jose. "Voter turnout in 2014 was the lowest since WWII." *Washington Post*, November 10, 2014.

DeWolf, Mary Louise. *A Cracker Gal Finds Religion*. Bloomington, IN: Author House, 2011.

Diamond, Jared. *Guns, Germs and Steel*. New York: W. W. Norton & Company, 1999.

Diamond, Jared. *Collapse*. New York: Viking Books, 2004.

Downey, Allen B. "Religious Affiliation, Education and Internet Use." *Cornell University Press*, March 12, 2014.

Einstein, Albert. *Living Philosophies*. New York: Simon and Schuster, 1931.

Epstein, Greg. *Good Without God: What a Billion Nonreligious People Do Believe*. New York: HarperCollins, 2009.

Evans, Robert (12/9/2013) *Atheists face death in 13 countries, global discrimination: study*. Reuters.

Exton, Reginald. *Make the Break (If You Can)*. Washington, DC: Humanist Press, 2013.

Fenton, Rory (3/30/2015) *Atheists are being hacked to death in Bangladesh, and soon there will be none left*. The Independent.

Galen, Luke W., Michael Sharp, and Alison McNulty (7/9/2014) "Nonreligious Group Factors Versus Religious Belief in the Prediction of Prosociality." *Social Indicators Research*, July 9, 2014.

Geisel, Theodore. *Happy Birthday To You By Dr. Seuss*. New York: Random House. 1959.

Goldstein, Rebecca. *Plato at the Googleplex: Why Philosophy Won't Go Away*. New York: Pantheon, 2014.

Granados, Luis. *Damned Good Company: Twenty Rebels Who Bucked the God Experts*. Washington, DC: Humanist Press, 2012.

Granados, Luis, and Roy Speckhardt, eds. *A Jefferson Bible for the Twenty-First Century*. Humanist Press, 2012.

Goudreau, Jenna. "Why Working Is The Secret To Happiness." *Forbes*, June 29, 2011.

Gunn, Jeremy, and John Witte, Jr. *No Establishment of Religion: America's Original Contribution to Religious Liberty*. Oxford, UK: Oxford University Press, 2012.

Hamann, Katharina et al. "Collaboration encourages equal sharing in children but not in chimpanzees." *Nature* 476 (2011): 328–331.

Harris Interactive. "Americans' Belief in God, Miracles and Heaven Declines." Accessed on December 16, 2013.

Harris, Sam. *Free Will*. New York: Free Press, 2012.

Harris, Sam. *The End of Faith*. New York: W.W. Norton & Company, 2004.

Harris, Sam. *Letter to a Christian Nation*. New York: Knopf, 2006.

Hirsi-Ali, Ayyan (3/23/2015) Interview with author of *Heretic*. The Daily Show with Jon Stewart.

Hitchens, Christopher. *God is Not Great: How Religion Poisons Everything*. Toronto, Ontario: McClelland and Stewart, 2007.

Isaacson, Walter. *Benjamin Franklin: An American Life*. New York: Simon and Schuster, 2003.

Jacoby, Susan. *Freethinkers: A History of American Secularism*. New York: Metropolitan Books, 2004.

Jáuregui, Pablo. "Entrevista Exclusiva Stephen Hawking 'No hay ningún dios. Soy ateo.'" *El Mundo*, September 21, 2014.

Jolie, Angelina. *Notes From My Travels*. New York: Simon and Schuster, 2003.

Kester, Grant H. *Art, Activism, and Oppositionality: Essays from Afterimage*. Durham, NC: Duke *University* Press Books, 1998.

Kaufman, Scott. "Salman Rushdie on Paris attack: Religion a 'medieval form of unreason' that deserves 'fearless disrespect.'" *Raw Story*, January 7, 2015.

Kohler, Pamela K, Lisa Manhart, and William Lafferty (2008) *Abstinence-Only and Comprehensive Sex Education and the Initiation of Sexual Activity and Teen Pregnancy*. Journal of Adolescent Health. Volume 42, Issue 4, 344-351.

Kurtz, Paul. "The McCarthyites of Virtue." *Free Inquiry*, Winter Issue, 1998-1999.

Lakoff, George. *Don't Think of an Elephant! Know Your Values and Frame the Debate*. White River Junction, VT: Chelsea Green Publishing, 2004.

Lamont, Corliss. *The Philosophy of Humanism*. Washington, DC: Humanist Press, 1997.

Lamont, Corliss. *Freedom Is As Freedom Does*. The Continuum Publishing Company, 1990.

Lucas, Sarah. "Free Will and the Anders Breivik Trial." *The Humanist*, September/October Issue, 2012.

Linaza, Jose. "Piaget's Marbles: the study of children's games and their knowledge of rules." *Oxford Review*, Vol. 10, No. 3 (1984).

Marantz Hang, Robert. "Darwin's God." *New York Times*, March 4, 2007.

Matthews, Dylan. "You give religions more than $82.5 billion a year." *Washington Post*, August 22, 2013.

McDonald, Henry. "Jesus wept … oh, it's bad plumbing. Indian rationalist targets 'miracles'." *The Guardian*, November 23, 2012.

McManimon, Michelle. "Sweat lodge ceremony revived." *Arizona Daily Sun*, December 11, 2014.

Mehta, Hemant. "Oprah Winfrey's Awkward Conversation with Marathon Swimmer Diana Nyad, an 'Atheist Who's in Awe.'" *The Friendly Atheist*, October 14, 2013.

Milk, Harvey. *An Archive of Hope: Harvey Milk's Speeches and Writings*. Oakland, CA: University of California Press, 2013.

Moeller, Philip. "Why Religion Is Linked With Better Health and Well-Being." *The Huffington Post*, April 15, 2012.

Mooney, Chris. "The Science of Why Cops Shoot Young Black Men." *Mother Jones*, December Issue, 2014.

Morain, Lloyd. *Humanism as the Next Step*. Washington, DC: Humanist Press, 2008.

Morales, Peter. "Science and the Search for Meaning." *The New Atlantis* Summer (2013): 119.

Niose, David. *Nonbeliever Nation: The Rise of Secular Americans*. New York: Palgrave Macmillan, 2012.

Pew Forum on Religion & Public Life. "U.S. Religious Landscape Survey." Pew Research Center, 2008.

Pinn, Anthony. *Writing God's Obituary*. Amherst, NY: Prometheus Books, 2014.

Pinker, Steven. *The Better Angels of Our Nature: Why Violence Has Declined*. New York: Viking Books, 2011.

Pinker, Steven; Andrew Mack (12/22/2014) *The World is Not Falling Apart*. Slate.

Post, Stephen G. "Altruism, Happiness and Health: It's Good to Be Good." *International Journal of Behavioral Medicine* Vol. 12, No. 2 (2005): 66-77.

Quinton, Matt. "Tragic Suicide of Woman Aged 105." *The Sun*, March 20, 2012.

Roy Morgan Research. "The Top 10 most popular newspaper sections on Monday to Friday, Saturday and Sunday." Accessed on August 14, 2013.

Sagnip, Jeff. "FEMA Continues to Discriminate Against Churches and Synagogues Devastated by Superstorm Sandy." *U.S. Congressman Chris Smith Website,* July 11, 2013.

Seltzer, Leon. "Justice Sonia Sotomayor's Empathy." *Psychology Today,* June 12, 2009.

Simpson, Lyle. *Why Was I Born?* Washington, DC: Humanist Press, 2014.

Snell, Marilyn Berlin. "The activist author of Alias Grace and The Handmaid's Tale discusses the politics of art and the art of the con." *Mother Jones*, July/August Issue, 1997.

Stack, Peggy Fletcher. "Mormon conversions lag behind huge missionary growth." *Salt Lake Tribune*, May 2, 2014.

Stedman, Chris. "How anti-atheist stigma affects the mental health of American nontheists." *Religion News Service*, June 14, 2014.

Steinem, Gloria. *Outrageous Acts and Everyday Rebellions*. New York: Henry Holt and Company, 1983.

Stiefel, Todd. "Why I Am Not a Catholic and Why I Am a Humanist." *Free Inquiry*, Vol. 34 Issue 2 (2014). Accessed January 14, 2014.

Strauss, Valerie. "Proposed Texas textbooks are inaccurate biased and politicized new report finds." *Washington Post*, September 12, 2014.

Tribble, Sarah Jane. "Measles Outbreak In Ohio Leads Amish To Reconsider Vaccines." *National Public Radio*, June 24, 2014.

Tyson, Neil deGrasse. "In Defense of the Big Bang." *Natural History*, December 2006/January 1997.

Uhl, Stephen. *Imagine No Superstition: The Power to Enjoy Life With No Guilt, No Shame, No Blame*. Oro Valley, AZ: Golden Rule Publishers, 2007.

Vonnegut, Kurt. *A Man Without A Country*. New York: Random House. 2007.

Weir, Kirsten. "Not-so Blank Slates." *Science Watch*. Vol. 45, No. 4 (2014).

Wine, Sherwin. *Staying Sane in a Crazy World*. Birmingham, MI: Center for New Thinking, 2005.

Wright, Richard. *Native Son*. New York: Harper and Brothers, 1940.

Yutang, Lin. *The Importance of Living*. New York: William Morrow and Company, 1937.

Zaimov, Stoyan. "Zach Dasher Stands by Comments on Atheism and Sandy Hook Massacre Following Richard Dawkins' Claim of 'Christian Intolerance'." *The Christian Post*, October 3, 2014.

Are You Good Without a God?
Join the Humanist Movement!

Become a member of the American Humanist Association! Help us further humanism by increasing our numbers and strengthening our voice.

Membership with the AHA includes a one-year subscription to the *Humanist* (6 issues) and the *Free Mind* newsletter (4 issues). Members also receive discounts to conferences and other special events. New members receive this book as a special bonus.

Your membership dues will support grassroots humanist advocacy in Washington and around the nation, as well as legal advocacy in defense of the First Amendment and humanists' rights. In addition, your membership will advance humanist education and scholarship and increase humanist visibility through national advertising and online communications.

Join the AHA today! Just fill in the form below and return to:

American Humanist Association
1777 T ST NW
Washington, DC 20009

Name: _____

Address: _____

Email: _____

Phone: _____

Credit Card Number: _____

Expiration Date:_____

Join online at www.americanhumanist.org or call 1-800-837-3792

ABOUT THE AUTHOR

Roy Speckhardt has served as executive director of the American Humanist Association since 2005. He is a frequent media commentator who has appeared on *Good Morning America, CNN Headline News, Fox News,* and *National Public Radio,* among others. He writes a regular column for *The Huffington Post* and has written for *Patheos, On Faith,* and other publications. He has spoken at universities from Stanford to Oxford, and given speeches at national conferences and local humanist-oriented groups across the United States.

Speckhardt also serves on the boards of The Institute for Humanist Studies, the United Coalition of Reason, The Humanist Institute, and the Secular Coalition for America Education Fund. He served as deputy director of the Interfaith Alliance from 1995 to 2001.

Speckhardt holds a Masters in Business Administration from George Mason University and a Bachelor of Arts in sociology from Mary Washington College. He currently lives and works in Washington, DC.